BE A BETTER

BE A BETTER LEADER

*Personality type and difference
in ministry*

Graham Osborne

First published in Great Britain in 2016

Society for Promoting Christian Knowledge
36 Causton Street
London SW1P 4ST
www.spck.org.uk

Copyright © Graham Osborne 2016

The author and publisher have made every effort to ensure that the external website
and email addresses included in this book are correct and up to date at the time
of going to press. The author and publisher are not responsible for the content,
quality or continuing accessibility of the sites.

British Library Cataloguing-in-Publication Data
A catalogue record for this book is available from the British Library

ISBN 978–0–281–07583–6
eBook ISBN 978–0–281–07854–3

Typeset by Graphicraft Limited, Hong Kong
First printed in Great Britain by Ashford Colour Press
Subsequently digitally printed in Great Britain

eBook by Graphicraft Limited, Hong Kong

Produced on paper from sustainable forests

Contents

Contents

Illustrations

Figures

Tables

Foreword

Christian theology and the science of psychology share a common interest and a common theme. Both are concerned with what it means to be human. As a consequence, the conversation between theology and psychology can enrich both disciplines, once they can come to agree on a shared starting point. The field of individual differences provides this.

This book is rooted in psychological type theory, and psychological type theory is rooted in the bigger field of the psychology of individual differences. The psychology of individual differences begins from the observation that people differ and that there are stable patterns in those differences. Psychological type theory identifies four such stable patterns. The theory speaks of stable differences in terms of orientation (extraversion[1] and introversion), ways of perceiving (sensing and intuition), ways of judging or evaluating (thinking and feeling) and ways of relating to the world (judging and perceiving). Psychological type theory conceives these differences as representing distinctive types and conceives each pair as equally good and equally acceptable. For example, an introvert is not a failed extravert, nor is an extravert an inadequate introvert.

The theology of individual differences looks at what it means to be human through the lens of Christian doctrine. The doctrine of creation affirms that human beings are created in the image of God (Genesis 1.27) and that God created diversity in God's creation by creating men *and* women in the divine image. According to the theology of Genesis 1.27, neither male nor female reflects less perfectly the image of the divine creator. Christian doctrine, however, places alongside the doctrine of creation the equally important doctrines of fall and redemption. By the fall the divine image has been corrupted, and by the saving work of Christ there has been offered the path to restoration. When looking at human beings, the theology of individual differences has to disentangle those differences rooted in creation and those rooted in the fall. Taking Genesis 1.27 seriously, sex differences are clearly rooted in creation: men and women are created equally in the image of God. By extension, the theology of individual differences argues that ethnic differences reflect the intention of the divine creator: black and white are created equally in the image of God. By extension, the theology of individual differences argues that psychological type differences reflect the intention of the divine creator: introverts and extraverts are created equally in the image of God.

Working within the tradition of the theology of individual differences, Graham Osborne invites clergy to take seriously and to accept responsibly the divine image in which they have been created: male or female; black or white; introvert or extravert; sensing type or intuitive type; thinking type or feeling type; judging type or perceiving type. With such acknowledgement comes the liberating joy of working with the resource that God has entrusted to us. The introvert will not do ministry in the same way as the extravert. Extraverts and introverts will excel at different things and struggle with different things. Different aspects of ministry will bring them joy or cause them exhaustion. But what is clear for the theology of individual differences is confidence that the God who creates difference also accepts difference.

In *Be a Better Leader*, Graham Osborne takes us on a well-informed and insightful journey to see more clearly the patterns that emerge within our individual psychological type profile and within the profiles of those with whom we work and among whom we minister. It is a journey well worth taking seriously.

Leslie J. Francis
Professor of Religions and Education, University of Warwick
Canon Theologian, Bangor Cathedral

Introduction

My main reason for writing this book is to explore the implications of psychological type theory for understanding the performance and experience of men and women engaged in professional Christian ministry. In the course of my work as a spiritual director, mostly with ordained and lay ministers, and in working as a Myers-Briggs® practitioner with Anglican and Methodist clergy, church staff teams and parochial church councils, I have observed that there are Christian ministers of all psychological types, both lay and ordained, and that they approach their Christian ministry in distinctive ways. Not only that but also that ministers with different psychological types find certain aspects of their ministry energizing and other aspects enervating; which is which depends on their particular type.

I first encountered the Myers-Briggs Type Indicator® (MBTI®) in the late 1980s, as a management consultant using a subset as part of a change-management methodology in implementing large computer systems. I then 'did it properly' in my firm in preparation for partnership and subsequently, having offered for ordination in 1994, in theological college. However, it was the report from the Society of Mary and Martha, *Affirmation and Accountability*, that sowed the seeds of my research in applying the MBTI to the exercise of Christian ministry.

That report, produced in 2002, highlighted that there is an issue with clergy stress. The report's subtitle is *The Society of Mary and Martha's Manual of Practical Suggestions for Preventing Clergy Stress, Sickness and Ill-health Retirement*. Section 2.3.2 contains the recommendation: 'Develop psychological profiling as a routine tool for cultivating self-awareness from selection onwards', and goes on to assert that psychometric tools, including the MBTI,

> can help the church to use its human resources more effectively by fitting the right clergy to the kind of job where they can flourish and work most effectively. They can help to provide useful information on the particular stresses people are likely to face in ministry, and help to pinpoint areas to be usefully addressed in training and formation.[1]

I was a member of the diocesan task group that sought to work out how the report's recommendations could be implemented in my then diocese, but sadly the cost of implementation meant that only a few of them made it beyond the cutting-room floor. It was not until a period of sabbatical leave in 2009 that I was able to return to the topic.

The theory of psychological types on which the MBTI is based was initially developed by Carl Gustav Jung, then further developed into a usable form by Katharine Cook Briggs and her daughter Isabel Briggs Myers. It proposes 16 complete types, each of which displays both characteristic strengths and characteristic weaknesses. When these strengths and weaknesses are projected on to the life experience and professional expectations of clergy, type theory suggests that each of the 16 types will display distinguishing characteristics.

The primary purpose of my research was to explore the implications of psychological type theory for understanding the performance and experience of men and women engaged in professional Christian ministry. The plan was to develop a profile for each of the 16 Myers-Briggs types, setting out the application of the Myers-Briggs theory to that type. In developing the shape of the profile, I asked myself four fundamental questions.

- For whom would I be developing the type profile?
- What end result was I hoping to achieve?

- If I were to develop a type profile that was 'fit for purpose', what would that purpose be?
- How would I measure how successful I had been in meeting that purpose?

I identified my target audience as any Christian minister exercising a public ministry, especially those in leadership. The resulting end-product would be a set of 16 documents, each containing the profile of one Myers-Briggs type – a type profile. The purpose would be to provide for a Christian minister a description of his or her type, a statement of those aspects of Christian ministry that, in theory, would be energy giving and life enhancing, those aspects that would tend to be draining and even stressful, and some strategies for avoiding, or lessening, the impact of these latter aspects. The measures of success would be, in the short term, validation by peer practitioners in the field and, in the medium term, validation by members of the target group. Longer-term validation would have to wait for the empirical field research that would be the subject of a further study.

This book is based on the research I undertook to develop these type profiles and documented in a thesis for which I was admitted by the University of Wales to the degree of Master of Philosophy. It was most affirming to have my research and its conclusions subjected to such academic rigour. My MPhil research concentrated on applying the theory; testing it would probably need to be a PhD study. As my wife spells 'PhD' 'D-I-V-O-R-C-E', I think that will have to be a retirement project.

The book is intended to enable people in Christian ministry to generate new insights into their own experience and performance, and to develop better strategies both for maximizing their strengths and for protecting themselves against inevitable consequences of recognized weaknesses.

How to use this book

The book is divided into two parts. In Part 1 I explore the thinking behind psychological type theory and its application to Christian ministry. Part 2 discusses in individual chapters the 16 detailed type profiles. For each type profile I begin with an introduction that gives the recognized characteristics of that type, and does so by setting out what are termed the type dynamics – the Dominant, Auxiliary, Tertiary and Inferior functions (these are explained in greater detail on p. 65). The second section within each profile chapter examines the 'comfort zone' for that type, expanding on that type's strengths. The third section explores what happens 'outside the comfort zone' and draws attention to some of the difficulties experienced by the type under discussion. The fourth section examines the 'stress response'. The fifth section discusses 'life-giving strategies'. Each chapter then concludes with a summary profiling the type.

Most readers of this book will probably already be aware of their type. However, for those who aren't I have included a questionnaire on p. 31. Alternatively, there are now many reliable tests available online, for example:

- <www.25quiz.com> by John Hawksley
- <www.humanmetrics.com/cgi-win/jtypes1.htm> by Catherine Elizabeth Valdes
- <www.41q.com/> by Chintan Pathak
- <http://careerassessmentsite.com> by Jimmy Mckenzie
- <www.onlinepersonalitytest> by Bogdan Vaida
- <www.typefocus.com> by Tara Orchard
- <http://similarminds.com/jung.html> by Jeff Haas
- <www.initforlife.com/home> by Sean Robert Greenhalgh
- <www.quistic.com/personali> by Cassie Boorn
- <www.16personalities.com> by Pieter-Christiaan Voorwinden.

Part 1

INTRODUCING PSYCHOLOGICAL TYPE THEORY

Psychological type theory

It would seem sensible to start with what psychological type is all about. If you would rather pass over the different theories and go straight to the type profiles, please feel free to go on to Part Two of this book, pausing at p. 31 if you would like to discover, or check, your own type.

The British Psychological Society defines 'psychology' as 'the science of mind and behaviour'. Psychology is a very wide field and my focus in this book is on personality psychology, so how does one define 'personality'? The definitions listed here are from both the academic world and generally available dictionaries.

- Gordon Allport, who focused his studies on psychologically healthy individuals: 'Personality is the dynamic organization within the individual of those psychophysical systems that determine his characteristic behavior and thought.'[1]
- Robert Stephen Weinberg and Daniel Gould in *Foundations of Sport and Exercise Psychology*: 'the characteristics or blend of characteristics that make a person unique'.[2]
- Oxford Dictionaries online: 'The combination of characteristics or qualities that form an individual's distinctive character'.
- The *Collins English Dictionary*: 'the sum total of all the behavioural and mental characteristics by means of which an individual is recognized as being unique'.
- Merriam-Webster online dictionary: 'the set of emotional qualities, ways of behaving, etc., that makes a person different from other people'.

- American Psychological Association: 'Personality refers to individual differences in characteristic patterns of thinking, feeling and behaving. The study of personality focuses on two broad areas: One is understanding individual differences in particular personality characteristics, such as sociability or irritability. The other is understanding how the various parts of a person come together as a whole.'[3]

This aspect of 'how the various parts of a person come together as a whole' is key to what this book is about – understanding how we 'come together as a whole' in order to lead most effectively out of who we really are. If we are to be as effective as possible as Christian leaders, we need to understand our own personalities and the strengths and weaknesses inherent in them in exercising our chosen vocation.

Before we go any further, there is a caveat – Leslie Francis, the priest, theologian and psychologist who wrote the Foreword to this book, draws a distinction in personality psychology between *personality* and *character*. The former he understands to be 'value neutral', lying 'at the heart of who we are . . . [describing] basic individual differences at a level of being over which we may have very little personal control';[4] the latter he understands to be 'heavily value laden' with a 'good' character exhibiting virtues and a 'bad' character vices.

Human beings have been striving for self-understanding for some considerable time. The inscription on the forecourt of the Temple of Apollo at Delphi reads 'Know Thyself', a saying attributed to, among others, Socrates. It could be argued that an understanding of personality is fundamental to the development of self. An improved knowledge of ourselves and others, in terms of motivation, strengths and weaknesses, and preferred thinking and working styles, can also lead to an understanding of our preferred style for communicating with others, for learning, for managing ourselves and others and working as part of a team. The more we understand about our own personality, and the personality of others, the better our understanding of how others respond to us, how they perceive us and how they react to our own personality and style of working.

Personality theories

A range of personality theories has developed over the centuries. The earliest personality type theory was arguably developed more than 5,000 years ago by the Egyptian and Mesopotamian civilizations. This characterized health in terms of the four elements of fire, water, earth and air, which began to be associated with certain organs in the body, bodily fluids and how to treat an imbalance of these.

The four temperaments or four humours can be seen in ancient Greek medicine and philosophy in the work of Hippocrates and Galen. Greek medical practice held that a healthy person needed a balance of the four bodily fluids of blood, phlegm, yellow bile and black bile. Hippocrates made the following attributions: blood characterized by cheerfulness, black bile by sombreness, yellow bile by enthusiasm and phlegm by calmness.

In his book *People Patterns: A Modern Guide to the Four Temperaments*,[5] Stephen Montgomery suggested that these four temperaments could be identified in the Bible in the prophet Ezekiel:

> The centre of the fire looked like glowing metal, and in the fire was what looked like four living creatures. In appearance their form was human, but each of them had four faces and four wings . . . Their faces looked like this: each of the four had the face of a human being, and on the right side each had the face of a lion, and on the left the face of an ox; each also had the face of an eagle. (Ezekiel 1.4–6, 10 NIV)

Montgomery suggested that there was a correlation between these animal characteristics and personality characteristics – the lion characterizes boldness, the ox sturdiness, the man humaneness and the eagle the characteristic of being far-seeing.

The Greek physician Galen developed the ideas of Hippocrates into the four humours, where he characterized these words of Hippocrates thus: cheerful became sanguine, sombre became melancholic, enthusiastic became choleric and calm became phlegmatic.

Daniel Nettle suggests that the story of personality psychology and its measurement starts with an 1884 article by Sir Francis Galton entitled 'The Measurement of Character'.[6] Galton was Charles Darwin's first cousin and an early proponent of the theory of evolution and its relevance to human beings. Regarding this theory of natural selection, Nettle would argue that it was Galton who first understood that studies of familial characteristics, in particular the study of twins, would be the means of unlocking what contribution nature and nurture made to the variations in human personality.

In the twentieth century, personality psychology developed into two main streams, those of *trait* and *type*. Those theories that focus on trait make a basic assumption that there are characteristics that are universal to all human beings, such as warmth, intellect, emotional stability, aggressiveness, the only difference being in the amount of the characteristic possessed. So those psychometric instruments that operationalize trait-based theories, such as the Five Factor Model or the 16PF, measure the quantity of a particular trait possessed by each human being.

Trait theory would argue that there is a standard distribution in a population such that the normal bell curve of a standard distribution – a normal distribution – shows the majority of people possess an average amount of any particular trait, with the smaller numbers being at the extreme ends. The argument would also continue that scores nearer the mean score would be deemed to be healthier than those at the extreme ends. So in a trait-based instrument, the score indicates the quantity of a particular trait possessed by an individual. A low score for 'warmth', for example, would indicate that the individual is cold and selfish, whereas a high score would indicate a supportive and comforting person; a low score for 'aggressiveness' would indicate modesty and docility, a high score someone who is controlling and tough. This is significant because traits are said to cause behaviour. That being so, the more of a particular trait an individual possesses, the more extreme the behaviour associated with that trait will be. It would then follow that an excess or dearth of a particular trait would be seen as negative. Trait theory argues that behaviours seem to be caused by the amount or the quantity of the trait possessed.

Type theories on the other hand refer to individuals possessing preferences that are qualitatively different one from another. So in type theory each element is a distinct dichotomy – either one or the other – not a continuum that places that element somewhere along a scale, plotting the quantity of that element. For example, the 'orientation' dichotomy will show an individual's preference for the source of his or her psychological energy – either from the outer world, Extraversion,[7] or from the inner world, Introversion. The 'perceiving' preference, how an individual prefers to acquire information, will either be for what can be gleaned using the five senses, Sensing, or for what can be picked up intuitively, iNtuition. Type theories, therefore, do not refer to a 'normal' distribution. The measurement in a type instrument does not indicate a quantity, merely a preference for one or other of the dichotomies. The strength of the score on a type instrument would indicate the clarity with which individuals understand that they have that preference or the confidence that they would have in expressing that preference.

In type theory, therefore, behaviour would tend to be an expression of the preference rather than being caused by it. In addition, a person who expresses a preference for one of the dichotomies can still use the other preference, the opposite preference, and therefore there is no implication of weakness or pathology in there being too much or too little of a preference. There is a tendency to think that a very slight preference for one element over the other tends to mean that one would be equally happy using either. While it is true that each individual can use all eight of the preferences, the analogy of the type 'Englishness' is helpful. Dover is geographically a lot closer to Calais than to Liverpool. However, the 'Englishness' of a Liverpudlian will be much more in tune with the girl from Dover than the 'Frenchness' of the lady who hails from Calais.

So 'type' language would tend to reflect intentional choice as an expression of the dichotomy choice.

David Keirsey (1921–2013) was an American educational psychologist turned academic who developed his own type instrument, the Keirsey Temperament Sorter, of which more in the next chapter. Keirsey traces the development of Galen's four temperaments into the temperament theory embedded in the Myers-Briggs Type Indicator®[8] (MBTI®) and in his own work on temperaments.[9] The trail continues with the work of the German philosopher Erich Adickes (1866–1928) and his four world views: dogmatic, agnostic, traditional and innovative; then to the German psychiatrist Ernst Kretschmer (1888–1964), who argued that there was a correlation between physique and character, suggesting that certain body types are associated with particular types of mental disorder. The trail continues after that with the four 'mistaken goals' defined by the Austrian psychiatrist Alfred Adler (1870–1937), recognition, power, service and revenge, and the four human values defined by the German philosopher and psychologist Eduard Spranger (1882–1963), religious, theoretic, economic and artistic.[10]

The temperament aspect of type theory contained in both the MBTI and Keirsey's Temperament Sorter have common roots (see Table 1).

Table 1 Roots of temperament theory

Galen	Myers-Briggs®	Keirsey
Sanguine	SP (Sensing Perceiving)	Artisan
Melancholic	SJ (Sensing Judging)	Guardian
Choleric	NF (iNtuition Feeling)	Idealist
Phlegmatic	NT (iNtuition Thinking)	Rationalist

I will go into more detail about the MBTI and the Keirsey Temperament Sorter in the next chapter.

Models of personality

When I was conducting my research I felt that it was important to cover the ground of how 'personality' is defined and measured in modern times, and therefore thought it right to look at the 'big hitters' in some detail. I discovered that there are two broad traditions within the field of personality psychology. The first concerns itself with abnormal psychological development and mental illness, rooted in clinical experience with practitioners such as Freud. The second is concerned with normal psychological development, seeking to categorize the normally developed psyche. It was beyond the scope of my research to go into the field of mental illness, so I concentrated on this second broad tradition, how the 'normal' psyche develops and is classified and measured.

The four best-established models of personality are three trait theories, those of Hans Eysenck with his three-dimensional model,[11] Paul T. Costa and Robert R. McCrae with their Five-Factor Model of Personality,[12] Raymond Cattell and his Sixteen Personality Factor (16PF) model;[13] and one type theory, Carl Gustav Jung's psychological type theory, first published in 1921.[14] I will now cover these four models in some detail.

Eysenck's P-E-N model

In his model of human personality, Eysenck makes two basic assumptions about its structure. The first is about the nature of mental illness, and posits that there is a clear continuum between psychological health and psychological pathology, seeing no fundamental distinction between normal and abnormal personality. His contention is that those who suffer from psychological illness will display a set of characteristics in a particularly concentrated form, those characteristics being present, more or less, within the healthy population. His second assumption is that the dimensions of personality, of which he understands there to be three main subdivisions, are totally independent of one another.

Eysenck's model – commonly referred to as the P-E-N model – has three independent dimensions, Psychoticism, Extraversion and Neuroticism. The model is a hierarchical one based on a behavioural predicate:

- a life situation will give rise to a specific response;
- a cluster of specific responses will constitute a habitual response;
- a cluster of habitual responses will constitute a trait;
- a cluster of traits will constitute a type.

The three independent dimensions – Psychoticism, Extraversion and Neuroticism – are at the highest level and are considered to be type variables or 'supertraits'. In their paper on trait measurement of the P, E and N supertraits,[15] Eysenck and his colleagues listed the traits contributing to each of the three factors (see Table 2).

Eysenck's insistence on the independence of these three dimensions means that a knowledge of the position a particular individual has on one dimension has no place in predicting the position that person would have on the other two dimensions.

Table 2 Traits comprising Eysenck's supertraits

P – Psychoticism	E – Extraversion	N – Neuroticism
Aggressive	Sociable	Anxious
Cold	Lively	Depressed
Egocentric	Active	Guilt feelings
Impersonal	Assertive	Low self-esteem
Impulsive	Sensation-seeking	Tense
Antisocial	Carefree	Irrational
Unempathetic	Dominant	Shy
Creative	Surgent	Moody
Tough-minded	Venturesome	Emotional

So in order to place an individual within the three-dimensional personality of Eysenck's model, scores for all three dimensions are required.

The Five-Factor Model

In his paper describing the emergence of the Five-Factor Model of personality structure,[16] John M. Digman considers that it was William McDougall, writing on character and personality in 1932, who anticipated a considerable amount of later research by identifying five distinguishable factors into which personality could be analysed: intellect, character, temperament, disposition and temper.

Subsequent research work by a number of other psychologists culminated in the inventory developed by Costa and McCrae. This was designed to measure personality across the following five factors: Neuroticism (N), Extraversion (E), Openness (O), Agreeableness (A) and Conscientiousness (C). In their validation study,[17] McCrae and Costa set out these five factors, each with a subset of facets describing the range of personality traits recorded. If you are interested, a list of descriptions can be found in course material from the University of Kentucky.[18]

Nettle[19] summarizes the personality dimensions thus:

- Extraversion – high scorers being described as outgoing and enthusiastic and low scorers as aloof and quiet;
- Neuroticism – high scorers being described as prone to stress and worry, low scorers as emotionally stable;
- Conscientiousness – high scorers being described as organized and self-directed, low scorers as spontaneous and careless;
- Agreeableness – high scorers being described as trusting and empathetic, low scorers as uncooperative and hostile;
- Openness to experience – high scorers being described as creative, imaginative and eccentric, low scorers as practical and conventional.

Nettle sees a congruence with these five personality dimensions not only in Cattell's five global traits but also with Eysenck's three supertraits of Extraversion, Neuroticism and Psychoticism if one sees this last factor as an amalgam of Agreeableness and Conscientiousness.

16PF

While he was at Harvard in the 1940s, Raymond Cattell set out to develop a comprehensive model of personality traits that would fully describe the human person. From a set of some 4,500 adjectives culled from an English dictionary that could describe a person, Cattell and his team used factor analysis to refine these down to 171 'clusters' and then to the 16 traits that they thought was the smallest number of factors that could describe observable human behaviour in the fullest terms. These were further refined by factor analysis to determine the five global traits into which they fall – Extraversion, Receptivity, Anxiety, Independence and Self-control. A personality inventory was then developed to measure the 16 traits. These are designated with alphabetic letters from A to I, L to O and four Qs, 1 to 4. If you are interested, the factors, their low- to high-score meanings, and example adjectival descriptors can be found online.[20] For those with a preference for pictures, the interrelationship between the 16 factors has been expressed diagrammatically (see Figure 1).

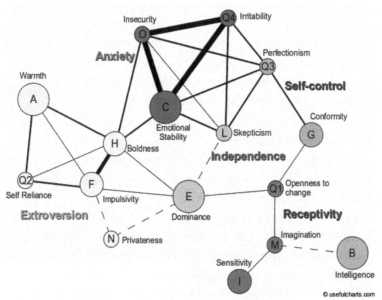

Figure 1 Cattell's 16PF – relationships between factors

Thicker lines represent stronger relationships. Data is based on intercorrelations reported in Samuel E. Krug (1981), *Interpreting 16pf Profile Patterns*, Champaign, IL: IPAT.

Carl Gustav Jung

Jung was a Swiss psychiatrist who is held by many to be, together with Sigmund Freud, one of the founding fathers of modern psychology. Jung's theory of typology was published in his book *Psychological Types* in 1921 in German and in 1923 in English translation. His theory of psychological type contains four main components. The first is the concept of *orientation*, focusing on the source of psychological energy. Those with a preference for introversion (I) derive their psychological energy from their internal resources, while those with a preference for extra-version (E) derive theirs from external sources.

The second and third components – human psychological 'processes' – are concerned with how an individual prefers first to acquire information (the *perceiving* process) and then to make decisions (the *judging* process). Each process is expressed through two opposing functions. The acquisition of informa-tion is either through sensing (S), using the five senses, or through intuition (N), 'hearing the music as well as the words'. The processing of information, evaluation and decision-making is either through logical, objective analysis, thinking (T), or through reference to its impact on others or how well it accords with an internal value system, feeling (F).

For Jung, the fourth component is the preferred *attitude* for the judging process or perceiving process, either in the outer world or the inner world. Whereas Jung would describe an individual as, for example, preferring Introverted iNtuition with Extraverted Thinking, those researchers who have built on Jung's theory have made explicit what Jung has kept implicit by adding a fourth component, judging (J) or perceiving (P). So preferring Introverted iNtuition with Extraverted Thinking would be expressed as INTJ.

It is worth noting that Jung's use of terminology was very specific; introversion and extraversion refer to the source of an individual's psychological energy, not to their social behaviours; judging and perceiving refer to an individual's preferred attitude to the outer world, not whether that individual is judgemental or perceptive.

As I have observed before, trait theories of personality – like the first three models of personality explored – tend not to be value-free in that they all include scales that can be construed as ranging from 'good' or desirable to 'bad' or undesirable character traits. Jungian typology, however, has no embedded value judgements – no 'good' or 'bad', merely 'different'. It is this fourth model that is frequently used in the course of training ordinands for life as Christian ministers and is consequently more familiar to those exercising Christian ministry than other models. It is the Jungian typology model on which this book will focus – it underpins the MBTI with which many ministers will already be familiar.

Assessing psychological type

It's all very well to have the Jungian typology model, but how do you measure it? Measuring any aspect of psychology comes under the general term 'psychometrics' – the design and use of psychological tests. Perhaps the most familiar is the IQ test, beloved of 11-plus examiners of old, and of HR departments and executive-placement consultancies of today for employment selection, personal and leadership development. You have only to enter 'psychometric test' into a search engine to discover the plethora of such tests available on the internet. If nothing else, the number and range of such tests indicate how hungry we human beings are to understand ourselves better.

When it comes to measuring psychological type, a number of tools exists. The MBTI® questionnaire, originally developed in the USA by Katharine Briggs and her daughter Isabel, was first published in 1943. Katharine had been inspired to look more deeply into personality type theory when she met Clarence Myers (who was to become her future son-in-law), because he viewed the world in a different way from her. She started reading widely on the subject of temperament theory and was struck by how similar her own theories were to those of Carl Jung as published in his book *Psychological Types*. It was primarily Isabel's work to devise a psychometric test to identify psychological type.

Over the years, various instruments designed to measure type have been developed, including the Gray-Wheelwright Jungian Type Survey, the Singer-Loomis Type Deployment Instrument (SL-TDI), the Personal Style Inventory, the Crosby

Type Indicator, the PET Check (Personal Empowerment through Type), the Personal Preferences Self-Description Questionnaire (PPSDQ) and the Francis Psychological Type Scales developed by Leslie Francis. Probably the best known of the temperament measurement tools is the Keirsey Temperament Sorter, now the Keirsey Temperament Sorter II.

As it is not the intention of this book to undertake a comparative study of type measurement instruments, I will look at three of the main ones in more detail – the Keirsey Temperament Sorter, the Francis Psychological Type Scales (FPTS) and the MBTI. Consideration of the MBTI will be taken to a further level of detail as it is the tool on which the main body of this book is based.

Criticisms of the MBTI

Before I go into detail about these three psychometric instruments, it would be prudent first to explore the main criticisms that have been levelled at type theory and at the MBTI in particular. These criticisms have been voiced in both secular and religious literature. First, a caveat: it is important to distinguish between the theory and the instrument used to apply it. There may be doubts expressed about the validity or reliability of the instrument; that should in no way discredit the theory that underlies it.

I would like to set out my own viewpoint as an MBTI practitioner before looking at the published work. The MBTI instrument has two versions for the practitioner: Step I, a typically paper-based exercise focused on the four fundamental dichotomies; and Step II, which is a typically computer-based exercise that drills down into each of the four preference pairs to refine those preferences with five supplementary subscales. In Step I, the four preference pairs are

- Extraversion–Introversion
- Sensing–Intuition
- Thinking–Feeling
- Judging–Perceiving

In Step II, the subscales are:

- **Extraversion–Introversion**
  - Initiating–Receiving
  - Expressive–Contained
  - Gregarious–Intimate
  - Active–Reflective
  - Enthusiastic–Quiet
- **Sensing–Intuition**
  - Concrete–Abstract
  - Realistic–Imaginative
  - Practical–Conceptual
  - Experiential–Theoretical
  - Traditional–Original
- **Thinking–Feeling**
  - Logical–Empathetic
  - Reasonable–Compassionate
  - Questioning–Accommodating
  - Critical–Accepting
  - Tough–Tender
- **Judging–Perceiving**
  - Systematic–Casual
  - Planful–Open-ended
  - Early starting–Pressure-prompted
  - Scheduled–Spontaneous
  - Methodical–Emergent

The evaluation of a psychometric instrument tends to be based on its standalone accuracy – the reliability and validity required being based on administering the test alone. By contrast, the whole process of helping somebody to understand themselves better using the MBTI is a consultative one. In my own practice for a Step I consultation, well before the feedback interview I will have sent out to my client the MBTI questionnaire, a scoring form and an explanatory leaflet with a covering letter. In the letter I invite the client to take half an hour, at home and relaxed, in a comfortable chair, possibly even with a glass of wine, and answer the 88 questions without overthinking the answers. The aim is to get an instinctive preference expressed.

At the feedback interview itself I will ignore the client's scoring form for the first half of the interview. I then describe each preference pair in some detail, with examples, and ask the client at the end of each pair how strongly he or she feels a preference for one over the other, and record the strength of preference. This process results in the client's 'self-assessed type'. Only then do we go to the scoring sheet to score the client's responses to the questionnaire. This then gives us a 'reported type', together with the strength with which each preference has been expressed. It should be noted that all the questionnaire can do is tell you how you answered it. If you answer the questionnaire by being conscious of what other people might think, especially your parents (dead or alive), or how unacceptable a particular response would be in your work environment, that will be reflected in your responses. Research shows that in some 75 per cent of cases, the questionnaire will accurately record preferences for three out of four of the dichotomies. The client and I will then explore together where there is a difference between self-assessed type and reported type. We will revisit the descriptions of the preferences in dispute and, it is hoped, resolve them into a 'best-fit type'. As far as I am concerned, our best-fit type is the closest we can get to our 'true type'. In his book *People Types and Tiger Stripes*, Gordon D. Lawrence explained true type like this:

Jung believed that each person has a true type that he or she may not yet have discovered. The true type does not change, although it may seem to, as one focuses on developing different mental processes at different stages of one's life. Behaviors can change, of course, but the roots of them remain the same. However, there are many reasons you might take the MBTI instrument two different times and come out as different types. You might still be discovering your preferences and trying them on for size. Or you might be working especially hard to develop one of the mental processes so that you report it on the MBTI instrument with stronger than usual emphasis. Or, you might take the MBTI instrument one time as your 'job self,' responding as you see yourself acting on the job, and you might take it another time as your 'home self,' responding as you see yourself in your home environment. If your type differs in two reports, this fact may lead to interesting information about yourself. As you cast your thoughts back to your frame of mind when you were answering the questions, consider how it may have affected your reporting of yourself and it may or may not reflect your true type.[1]

Turning now to the criticisms, I will take the secular literature first. Rowan Bayne, in his book *The Myers-Briggs Type Indicator®: A Critical Review and a Practical Guide*,[2] sets out, and responds to, the five main criticisms of type theory and of the MBTI.

1 The first criticism is that type and MBTI results are an insult to individuality – that type 'puts people in boxes', labels and stereotypes. His reply is that type and MBTI do not attempt to capture individuality but offer a broad framework within which people can move towards appreciating individuality. He asserts that type suggests four of the most important points on which personalities differ – what Jung described as 'compass points in the wilderness of the psyche'.

2 The second criticism is that behaviour is different in different situations, that people are flexible persons, not automata, and that part of being fully human is to choose which self

to be in a given situation. Bayne's reply is that most behave as if personalities exist. He then refers to the body of research that has shown that particular behaviours are consistent over time, that different behaviours tend to cluster together and that situations do have an effect but that a person's behaviour can be predicted on average.

3 The third criticism is that the type descriptions are too vague and general, such that most people would be able to see themselves in most or at least several of them. In response, Bayne argues that this criticism may misunderstand what the descriptions are intending to achieve. Given the almost infinite variety of individuals it would be demonstrably impossible to distil an individual down to a single paragraph. However, type descriptors can assist individuals to assess their own preferred way of functioning – not asserting who and how they are, but helping them to increased self-awareness.

4 The fourth criticism is that the MBTI report form descriptions are too positive, one of Bayne's colleagues describing them as 'vignettes of unrelenting virtue' – flattery rather than accuracy. Bayne's reply is threefold: that the type descriptions are not intended to encompass the whole of a personality but to set out some broad themes; that there is often a 'twist' in the type descriptions so that they are not unrelentingly positive; that the positive nature of the MBTI report form has great value in that some topics are very sensitive, so that a positive 'spin' can be perceived as non-threatening and constructive.

5 The fifth criticism is that the MBTI type descriptions miss out important aspects of Jung's theory. There are two aspects to this criticism. The first is by Angelo Spoto, namely that MBTI has 'broken away from Jung' and is developing independently. The second, by A. M. Garden, is that MBTI diverges from Jung in four issues in Myers' theory. In responding to Spoto's criticism, based on the argument that the

unconscious is much more influential than the MBTI literature would acknowledge and than the measurement tool allows, Bayne refers to the validity of the MBTI instrument – of which more later – and the accuracy with which type can be observed, arguing that the unconscious in fact is much less influential than Spoto asserts. In response to Garden's fourfold criticism, Bayne has a threefold response. Garden's first two criticisms centre on the introduction of a fourth aspect of type: an individual's preference for using either the perceiving function or the judging function, their attitude to the outer world. Garden raises two detailed questions about the Judging/Perceiving attitude; Bayne responds that the Judging/Perceiving attitude identifies a valuable individual difference in its own right and that the type descriptions do in fact embody the ideas Garden criticizes, and that they are reasonably accurate.

The third of Garden's criticisms questions whether everybody actually *is* a type. Bayne's reply is that, despite some people being hard to type accurately, Myers' theory can cope with such difficulty as, empirically, people seem to be happy with being either one or the other of each dichotomy. Bayne quotes Robert R. McCrae after his longitudinal research on five-factor theory: 'Barring such events as dementia and major depressive episodes, stable individual differences in basic personality traits are a universal part of human nature.'[3] Garden's fourth criticism echoes that of Spoto in that he questions whether the MBTI should be used outside the context of Jungian theory; the focus in MBTI on the behavioural, conscious and cognitive aspects of Jungian theory seems to Garden largely to ignore the unconscious. In response, Bayne sees these aspects of MBTI to be positive strengths while agreeing with Garden that there are indeed fundamental differences between Myers' theory and the MBTI, and Jung's theory. Again seeing those differences to be strengths, he goes on to assert that Myers' theory and the MBTI are 'far better supported empirically than Jungian theory, though still of course with much to clarify, test and refine'.[4]

In his 2012 paper in the *Journal of Beliefs and Values*,[5] John Lloyd analysed and evaluated what he termed the 'unresolved hostility' from the professional psychology community. He refers to a paper published in 1989 by McCrae and Costa that concluded 'that MBTI had no advantages, and some major drawbacks', and urged MBTI practitioners 'to abandon its Jungian framework and reinterpret the MBTI in terms of the five-factor model'.[6] 'This conclusion, by prominent and respected researchers, may largely explain the apparent dismissal of MBTI from serious consideration by the professional psychology community over the past two decades.' The conclusion in Lloyd's paper points a possible way forward:

> The understanding and analysis of human personalities are remarkably similar. They both postulate four major factors which, although given different names, denote closely similar qualities ... The similarities between the type and trait approaches to personality analysis are already very great. If each side could relinquish one of their cherished underpinnings, recognising its innate implausibility, there would be little to distinguish the two approaches and nothing to prevent an amicable and fruitful dialogue and the final resolution of a long-standing hostility.[7]

Turning to the religious literature, Leslie Francis in his book *Faith and Psychology*[8] sets out a helpful analysis of the criticisms contained in Kenneth Leech's collection of eight essays, *Myers-Briggs: Some Critical Reflections*.[9] His conclusion is that all eight essayists tended to misrepresent and misinterpret the way type theory is applied in a church-related context. Francis identifies three threads running through the eight essays:

1 that psychological type can be misused by churches;
2 that relying on psychological type theory places Christian spirituality in a psychological as opposed to a theological context;
3 that human personality is inherently too complex to be assessed by psychometric tests, such tests degrading and undervaluing each individual's uniqueness.

To the first thread, Francis responds that psychological type theory can indeed be misused in churches and argues that this is the reason why it is imperative that those who seek to apply the richness of psychological type theory are trained and equipped in both psychological type and in theology. Ideally the response to this criticism should be improved practice rather than dismissal of the theory and the tools.

The second thread of criticism appears to misunderstand the ways practitioners trained in both psychological type theory and in theology seek to synthesize the two in practice. In spiritual direction practice, the insights afforded by psychological type theory provide a rich resource for assisting directees in the development of their prayer lives and their spirituality and, indeed, on their journey towards individuation – defined by Jung in his *Psychological Types* as

> the process by which individual beings are formed and differentiated; in particular, it is the development of the psychological individual as a being distinct from the general, collective psychology. Individuation, therefore, is a process of differentiation, having for its goal the development of the individual personality.[10]

One could characterize this as the journey towards our true type. Francis argues for understanding and appreciation of the 'proper application of psychological methods and theories within the discipline of theology itself'.[11]

To the third criticism regarding the complexity of human personality being somehow degraded and undervalued, Francis responds:

> Such an accusation dismisses the enterprise of modern psychology, assumes that creation itself is random, and questions the fundamental principle of seeking scientifically discernible patterns underpinning the created universe. Such challenges may be too ambitious to sustain.[12]

In her January blog on how to respond to criticism of the MBTI assessment,[13] Dr Penny Moyle writes:

> Although various pieces have been written to refute and re-explain the different criticisms of the MBTI instrument, there is actually something enormously powerful about the experience that we are able to deliver as practitioners, and this is often our most convincing argument.

Measurement tools

Having taken a look at the criticisms of Jungian typology theory, and of the MBTI, I can now turn to a more detailed examination of three of the measurement tools in current use. I will start with the Keirsey Temperament Sorter (KTS). This was initially developed in the 1970s by David Keirsey and Marilyn Bates.[14] Keirsey subsequently revised the questionnaire as the Keirsey Temperament Sorter II.[15] The sorter, which is available in either paper and pencil or electronic form, comprises a 70-question forced-choice questionnaire, each question containing a pair of adjectives or phrases. For example, '2. Are you more (a) realistic or (b) philosophically inclined?' in the KTS; '2. Are you more (a) observant than introspective or (b) introspective than observant?' in the KTS II.

The choice of option is entered on an answer sheet that comprises a 14 × 10 matrix with the choice pairs comprising seven column pairs and the question numbers the ten rows, each row containing the answers to seven questions. Once all the answers have been recorded, the columns are totalled and the resulting total entered into pairs of boxes, one pair each for the Extraversion–Introversion, Sensing–Intuition, Thinking–Feeling and Judging–Perceiving scores. Ten questions determine the E-I score, with twenty questions each for the other three dichotomies. The resulting four-letter designation is one of the 16 MBTI types. A description of the type can then be provided by the administrator of the test.

For Keirsey, which of the 16 types an individual reports as is less important than the temperament within which that type falls: 'The real usefulness of the types comes not in memorizing the 16 portraits, but in understanding the temperamental base of the types.'[16] As he observed in his revised version:

> I soon found it convenient and useful to partition Myers' sixteen types into four groups, which she herself suggested in saying that all four of what she referred to as 'NFs' were alike in many ways and that all four of the 'NTs' [etc.] were alike in many ways – although what she called the 'STs' seemed to me to have very little in common, just as the 'SFs' had little in common. However, four earlier contributors, Adickes, Spränger, Kretschmer and Fromm, each having written of four types of character, helped me to see that Myers' four 'SJs' were very much alike, as were her four 'SPs'. Bingo! Typewatching from then on was a lot easier, the four groups – SPs, SJs, NFs and NTs – being light years apart in their attitudes and actions.[17]

In 1978 Keirsey and Bates named the four temperaments after characters in Greek mythology:

- the Sensing–Perceiving preference as the Dionysian temperament;
- the Sensing–Judging preference as Epimethean;

- the iNtuition–Thinking preference as Promethean;
- the iNtuition–Feeling preference as Apollonian.

In 1998 Keirsey renamed the four temperaments using Plato's categories of Artisan, Guardian, Rational and Idealist respectively, with the following characters defined:

- Artisans
  - The Promoter [ESTP]
  - The Crafter [ISTP]
  - The Performer [ESFP]
  - The Composer [ISFP]
- Guardians
  - The Supervisor [ESTJ]
  - The Inspector [ISTJ]
  - The Provider [ESFJ]
  - The Protector [ISFJ]
- Rationals
  - The Field Marshal [ENTJ]
  - The Mastermind [INTJ]
  - The Inventor [ENTP]
  - The Architect [INTP]
- Idealists
  - The Teacher [ENFJ]
  - The Counsellor [INFJ)
  - The Champion [ENFP]
  - The Healer [INFP]

In their review of the reliability of the KTS, Leslie Francis, Charlotte Craig and Mandy Robbins found that 'From the studies surveyed it may be concluded that the KTS indices are generally internally consistent.'[18]

Writing about temperament theory, Isabel Briggs Myers asserted that 'Temperament theory is widely used in connection with the MBTI. Though Jungian type and temperament are based on different assumptions and models of personality, they can complement each other. The MBTI gives access to both.'[19] She designates the temperaments as does Keirsey: NFs as Idealists, NTs as Rationals, SPs as Artisans and SJs as Guardians.

The MBTI is based on Briggs and Myers' interpretation of Jung's theory, sorting people into types rather than measuring traits. It comprises a forced-choice format with both phrase questions and word pairs. The standard form used in the USA is Form G and contains 94 questions, while the standard in the UK is the European English Step I questionnaire that contains 88 questions. The questionnaire is self-scorable, template-scorable and computer-scorable, with the preference scores reflecting the clarity of the reported preference. There are several research studies that examine the reliability and validity of the MBTI, notably Betsy Kendall, Sally Carr, Penny Moyle and Leanne Harris in the *MBTI® User's Guide* and Narender Kumar Chadha in *Applied Psychometry*, which conclude that it is both valid and reliable.[20] Chadha states that 'MBTI is a very popular test and more than three million people are administered MBTI each year . . . It has been used to study areas like communication, conflict, leadership, change, customer relations, and so on.'[21]

Considering the tools used to measure psychological type within a religious context, Francis explores what he terms the 'key psychometric properties' of reliability and validity:

> Reliability concerns the extent to which a psychological tool produces a consistent reading of whatever it is that the tool measures. Validity concerns the extent to which a psychological tool actually measures what it sets out to measure. A highly reliable instrument may not, however, necessarily be a valid instrument.[22]

In examining the MBTI, Francis refers to the study by Francis and Jones that concluded 'there was good evidence for internal consistency reliability and construct validity of the continuous scale scores, but that the use of the instrument to distinguish between discrete type categories remained considerably more problematic.'[23] The same study argued that 'some further refinement of the MBTI, giving particular attention to reassessing or reviewing those items which failed to achieve a corrected item total correlation of at least +0.30, would enhance the psychometric properties of the instrument.'

Further work on the psychometric properties of the MBTI, alongside Eysenck's three-dimensional model of human personality, was undertaken by Leslie Francis, Charlotte Craig and Mandy Robbins and concluded that 'the data demonstrated a number of statistically significant relationships between the two models of personality'.[24] Francis goes on to highlight the disadvantages of the MBTI as a research tool, and characterizes it as 'cumbersome' for research purposes, especially in studies where a large research sample is used. He also points up shortcomings in the KTS as an instrument for research purposes, being designed principally for self-assessment, and raises questions about the accuracy with which it assigns to type categories. In 2005 he therefore designed and published his own operationalization of Jungian psychological type theory specifically for research purposes: the Francis Psychological Type Scales (FPTS).

The FPTS comprise a 40-question, forced-choice questionnaire that uses both phrase questions and word pairs. As Francis explains:

> the Francis Psychological Type Scales were designed to present ten pairs of items to differentiate each of the four choices between extraversion and introversion, between sensing and intuition, between thinking and feeling, and between judging and perceiving. The four sets of ten items were then jumbled up so that the purpose behind each pair of items was not too transparent.[25]

Francis notes that 'a small but growing body of literature is now reporting on the psychometric properties of this new instrument'.[26] Among these is the study by Bruce Fawcett, Leslie Francis and Mandy Robbins that inter alia sums up the positioning of the three instruments described above by stating that

> The Myers-Briggs Type Indicator was designed for administration and interpretation by specially trained and licensed practitioners and is especially helpful in one-on-one consultations. The Keirsey Temperament Sorter was designed for self-completion and is especially helpful in exercises of self-examination. The Francis Psychological Type Scales were specifically designed for research purposes and are particularly useful in large-scale surveys in which participation is generally anonymous and the participants anticipate no individual feedback.[27]

It can be concluded, then, that the MBTI is a reliable and valid instrument for helping an individual to determine his or her psychological type, given guidance by a trained and experienced practitioner. In the training to become a registered practitioner, it is asserted that an individual is assisted to make a journey through four types. The first is the self-assessed type, chosen by an individual after hearing an exposition of the four dichotomies. The second is the reported type, the result from the questionnaire. The third type is the best-fit type, after resolution of any mismatches between the first two types. The fourth type is what Jung termed the true type, of which the best-fit type is an individual's current closest approximation. It may not be possible to determine an individual's type in a single consultation, so there may be a period of reflection and 'living with' the (usually) two types until the individual settles for the type that fits most comfortably.

It should be noted that each individual inhabits his or her type uniquely, while having something, or a lot, in common with others of the same type. MBTI trainers quote Isabel Briggs

Myers: 'an INFP is like all other INFPs, like some other INFPs and like no other INFP'.

Regardless of the qualities of the instrument, the MBTI comprises a rich resource of psychological type theory that can help individuals understand themselves and understand others, and provides a base for lifelong personality development so that they may become the best version of who they truly are – what Jung termed 'individuation'. Using that rich resource, this book now goes on to apply that theory to the exercise of Christian ministry.

NOTE: in case you have never discovered your psychological type, would like to check your understanding of your type or would just like a refresher, Leslie Francis has given me permission to include his type scales as a resource (see Figure 2).

Type questionnaire

If you do not know your Myers-Briggs® type, you are unsure of it or would like to check, please do complete the 40 questions in Figure 2 (overleaf). Try to be as relaxed as possible and answer instinctively by ticking one of the two boxes for each pair; try not to 'overthink' things or be influenced by 'what people might say', especially your parents or bosses.

How to use the questionnaire

In the following questionnaire there are four sections:

1 orientation
2 perceiving process
3 judging (evaluating) process
4 attitude.

Each section offers ten pairs of options; please tick one of each pair.

The following list contains pairs of characteristics. For each pair, tick
(✓) **ONE** box next to that characteristic which is **closer** to the real you,
even if you feel both characteristics apply to you. Tick the characteristic
that reflects the real you, even if other people see you differently.

PLEASE COMPLETE EVERY QUESTION

ORIENTATION

Do you tend to be more . . .

active	☐ or ☐	reflective

Are you more . . .

sociable	☐ or ☐	private

Do you prefer . . .

having many friends	☐ or ☐	a few deep friendships

Do you . . .

like parties	☐ or ☐	dislike parties

Are you . . .

energized by others	☐ or ☐	drained by too many people

Are you . . .

happier working in groups	☐ or ☐	happier working alone

Do you tend to be more . . .

socially involved	☐ or ☐	socially detached

Are you more . . .

talkative	☐ or ☐	reserved

Are you mostly . . .

an extravert	☐ or ☐	an introvert

Do you . . .

speak before thinking	☐ or ☐	think before speaking

PERCEIVING PROCESS

Do you tend to be more . . .

interested in theories	☐ or ☐	interested in facts

Are you more . . .

inspirational	☐ or ☐	practical

Do you prefer . . .

the abstract	☐ or ☐	the concrete

Do you . . .

prefer to design	☐ or ☐	prefer to make

Are you . . .

inventive	☐ or ☐	conventional

Do you tend to be more . . .

concerned for meaning	☐ or ☐	concerned about details

Are you more . . .

imaginative	☐ or ☐	sensible

Are you mostly focused on . . .

future possibilities	☐ or ☐	present realities

Do you prefer to . . .

improve things	☐ or ☐	keep things as they are

Are you . . .

up in the air ☐ or ☐ down to earth

JUDGING (EVALUATING) PROCESS

Do you tend to be more . . .

concerned for justice ☐ or ☐ concerned for harmony

Are you more . . .

analytic ☐ or ☐ sympathetic

Do you prefer . . .

thinking ☐ or ☐ feeling

Do you . . .

tend to be firm ☐ or ☐ tend to be gentle

Are you . . .

critical ☐ or ☐ affirming

Do you tend to be more . . .

logical ☐ or ☐ humane

Are you more . . .

truthful ☐ or ☐ tactful

Are you mostly . . .

sceptical ☐ or ☐ trusting

Do you . . .

seek for truth ☐ or ☐ seek for peace

Are you . . .

fair-minded ☐ or ☐ warm-hearted

ATTITUDE

Do you tend to be more . . .

happy with routine ☐ or ☐ unhappy with routine

Are you more . . .

structured ☐ or ☐ open-ended

Do you prefer . . .

to act on decisions ☐ or ☐ to act on impulse

Do you . . .

like to be in control ☐ or ☐ like to be adaptable

Do you tend to be more . . .

orderly ☐ or ☐ easygoing

Are you more . . .

organized ☐ or ☐ spontaneous

Are you mostly . . .

punctual ☐ or ☐ leisurely

Do you . . .

like detailed planning ☐ or ☐ dislike detailed planning

Are you . . .

happier with certainty ☐ or ☐ happier with uncertainty

Are you . . .

systematic ☐ or ☐ casual

Figure 2 Francis Psychological Type Scales (FPTS)

Table 3 Scoring sheet for FPTS

	L R		Please circle the letter with the higher score
Orientation	☐ ☐	L = **E**xtraversion R = **I**ntroversion	E I
Perceiving process	☐ ☐	L = i**N**tuition R = **S**ensing	N S
Judging (evaluating) process	☐ ☐	L = **T**hinking R = **F**eeling	T F
Attitude	☐ ☐	L = **J**udging R = **P**erceiving	J P

Scoring the questionnaire

When you have answered all 40 questions, please use Table 3 to record your scores. For each section, add up the total number of ticks in the left-hand column and enter that number in the left-hand box then add up all the ticks in the right-hand column and enter that total in the right-hand box.

If you have equal scores in any pair, add one to the score for I, N, F or P – and deduct one from the score for E, S, T or J. You should end up with four letters that represent your type according to the preferences you expressed in your answers.

Discovering the type profile of Christian leaders

There is a significant body of work that continues to develop the use of psychological type theory to produce profiles of ordained and lay leaders engaged in the practice of Christian ministry. There is also the Network for Psychological Type and Christian Faith, which holds a symposium every autumn that provides an opportunity for academic researchers as well as practitioners and trainers in psychological type to meet and share wisdom from their respective fields.[1] The symposium has been enriched in the past three years by the contribution of Phra Nicholas Thanissaro, a Buddhist priest who has shared his doctoral research into psychological type among young Buddhists. The purpose of this chapter is to pull together a number of these studies, in chronological order, to see if any conclusions emerge.

Leslie Francis, John Payne and Susan Jones focused on male Anglican clergy in Wales. They found that all 16 psychological types were represented in their sample of 427, and that there were two predominant types – 20 per cent Dominant Introverted Sensing with Extraverted Feeling (ISFJ) and 13 per cent Dominant Extraverted Feeling with Introverted Sensing (ESFJ). They concluded that

> the clerical profession, as developed and shaped within the Church in Wales, is diverse and embraces a wide range of activities and functions. Knowledge of the psychological types of Church in Wales clergy may help to predict the areas of

ministry most compatible with the preferences of the majority of clergy.[2]

Leslie Francis and Mandy Robbins moved away from studying only Anglican clergy in their study of evangelical church leaders. In the sample of 57 leaders, all 16 types were again represented. Taken together, two types predominated (ISFJ and ESFJ), accounting for 28 per cent of those responding to the type questionnaire. The study articulated the strengths that characteristics of these two types would bring to pastoral ministry, including 'warm, pastoral hearts . . . [loving] the people whom they are called to serve'. It also highlighted certain weaknesses to which they might be subject, including inflexibility and stubbornness, '[blindness] to the advantages of change and development' and reluctance 'to confront disagreement, to handle conflict, and to apply logical analysis to tough decisions'.[3]

To address the issue of individual differences between clergy in the way they exercise their various ministries, Leslie Francis and John Payne set out to build on previous work reflecting on the variety of roles or functions fulfilled by clergy.[4] Their method was to use the MBTI alongside a new instrument, the Payne Index of Ministry Styles (PIMS), to characterize preferred ministry styles using the eight elements of the MBTI dichotomies – Extraversion–Introversion, Sensing–iNtuition, Thinking–Feeling and Judging–Perceiving. They concluded that

> this analysis . . . has indicated the ability of this conceptualisation of ministry styles to illuminate individual differences in ministry preferences in light of psychological type theory [within which context] a coherent account has been advanced to explain two issues: the interrelationships between the eight indices of ministry style; and the relationships between the eight indices of ministry style and the eight

continuous scale scores proposed by the Myers-Briggs Type Indicator.[5]

This was a key indicator that further study of these indices of ministry style would be valuable in considering the exercise of Christian ministry by individuals with different personality type profiles.

Charlotte Craig, Tony Horsfall and Leslie Francis found two predominant types in their sample of 92 male evangelical missionary personnel training in England: ESTJ (24 per cent) and ISTJ (15 per cent).[6] Despite the small sample size, some provisional conclusions were formulated about their psychological preferences. The more frequent preference for Thinking over Feeling than in the general UK population led to the provisional conclusion that 'Thinking type men may be attracted to leadership roles within the evangelical tradition due to its emphasis on justice, truth and clear doctrine.'[7] The sample contained representatives of 15 of the 16 types, with no one reporting INFJ. The characteristics of those with the STJ preference were briefly reviewed in the light of the ministerial functions that might be strengths and those with which they might struggle – practicality versus visionary innovation, tough decision-making versus sensitivity and tact, orderly planning versus spontaneity and flexibility. The predominance of the SJ temperament was consistent with findings from other samples of male evangelical seminarians. The potential strength of this temperament was identified as a 'disciplined commitment to structure, detail and routine', with the corresponding potential weakness of 'inflexibility, resistance to change, and unwillingness to compromise on small details to achieve wider goals.'[8]

Leslie Francis, Charlotte Craig, Tony Horsfall and Christopher Ross widened the evangelical net by studying a sample of 322 evangelical lay church leaders in England, 192 female and 130 male, comparing them with UK population norms.[9]

Both male and female samples reported all 16 types, with ESFP as the lowest occurrence among the male leaders (1.5 per cent) and ESTP as the lowest among the female leaders (1.6 per cent). The study supported the conclusion of the developing body of research that different categories of church leader show significant variations in psychological type, both in gender differentiation and differences between lay and ordained ministers.

Anglican clergy in England were the focus for the study by Leslie Francis, Charlotte Craig, Michael Whinney, David Tilley and Paul Slater.[10] This too found that there were representatives of each of the 16 types among both the 626 male and the 237 female clergy, but found different predominant types – INTJ (11 per cent), INFP (10 per cent) and ISTJ (10 per cent) for male clergy; ENFJ (15 per cent), INFP (14 per cent) and ISFJ (12 per cent) for female clergy. In exploring the implications of these type preferences for both ministerial formation and the practical exercise of ministry, the preferences expressed for Introversion, iNtuition, Feeling and Judging were examined with reference to various aspects of the exercise of ministry, speculating that there may be some aspects that energize and some that enervate. For example, for clergy with a preference for Introversion, private study, counselling and silent prayer may be energizing, while attending social events, spontaneous public speaking and parish visiting may be draining. It was also observed that the research into the psychological type profile of church congregations indicates that three of the four preferences are shared – Introversion, Feeling and Judging – but that, while clergy predominantly prefer iNtuition, congregations predominantly prefer Sensing. The implications of 'Sensing types led by an iNtuitive cleric' highlighted the possibilities and likely areas of conflict. This reinforces the need for a deeper understanding of how type might affect the exercise of ministry.

Nearly half of the 81 male evangelical seminarians in the study by Leslie Francis, Charlotte Craig and Angela Butler[11] reported a similar preference for the SJ temperament (49 per cent), with ISTJ (19 per cent) and ESFJ (17 per cent) predominating. Only 14 of the 16 types were represented in this sample, the absentees being ISFP and INFP. Reference was made to the seven areas of potential difficulties for the SJ minister identified by Oswald and Kroeger[12] – literalism, pessimism, burnout, excessive rules and regulations, judgementalism, failure to appreciate others and intolerance of mavericks.

William Kay and Leslie Francis found that the predominant types reported by seminarians at the British Assemblies of God Theological College were ESTJ (18 per cent) and ISTJ (16 per cent).[13] There were no absentee types in this sample of 190, all 16 being represented. However, in contrast to the profiles of Anglican clergy found in the 2007 study by Francis, Craig, Whinney, Tilley and Slater referenced above, and the 2010 study by Leslie Francis, Mandy Robbins, Bruce Duncan and Michael Whinney,[14] where it predominates, the smallest representation in this study was of the INTJ type (2.1 per cent). The preference for Thinking over Feeling in this study identified its potential strengths in discernment, solving moral problems, tough-mindedness and self-discipline. Its potential weaknesses were also highlighted – 'adherence to principles of justice and truth, without due consideration of mercy and compassion'. The implications for intra-church and inter-church relationships, and for relationships with non-churchgoers, were also drawn out.

In exploring the implications of psychological type for preachers in their book *Preaching With All Our Souls: A Study in Hermeneutics and Psychological Type*, Leslie Francis and Andrew Village expanded on the potential strengths and difficulties of the predominant preferences in exercising a clerical

Christian ministry, highlighting the value of self-knowledge in religious professionals.[15]

In their study of Lead Elders within the Newfrontiers network of churches in the UK, Leslie Francis, Sean Gubb and Mandy Robbins found that the most frequently reported types were ISTJ (16 per cent) and ESTJ (13 per cent), contrasting with male Church of England clergy, whose most frequently reported types were INTJ (11 per cent) and ISTJ (10 per cent).[16] Again, some important strengths and potential weaknesses were highlighted: a slight preference for Extraversion inclining towards the building of a 'social church', a slight preference for Thinking attracting more men and Thinkers into membership, a preference for Sensing, being closer to the UK population profile, likely to be more attractive to a larger number, and a preference for Judging likely to lead to tight structures, close supervision and firm control. While this style of leadership can tend to plough on in the face of opposition, it can lead to hurt and marginalization for some individuals. As the study observes:

> It is, however, precisely the awareness of the implications of type preferences for leadership styles that can enable the continuing professional development of Lead Elders to become increasingly aware not only of the strengths that they bring to ministry but also of the dangers and weaknesses that they may face in exercising this personal strength.[17]

The sample of 622 male Anglican clergy in the 2010 study by Francis, Robbins, Duncan and Whinney noted above confirmed the four predominant preferences of Introversion over Extraversion, iNtuition over Sensing, Feeling over Thinking and Judging over Perceiving, but found that the predominant types were INFJ (15 per cent) and INTJ (15 per cent).[18] Contrasting the INFJ clergyman with the most predominant UK male, ISTJ, the observation made was 'with such different perspectives on life, Anglican clergymen and the general male population of the UK . . . may well seem to be occupying different planets.'[19] Again, the need for a deeper understanding of how ministry is exercised by different psychological types is highlighted.

The study by Leslie Francis, Michael Whinney, Lewis Burton and Mandy Robbins[20] of male and female Free Church ministers in England (Methodists and Baptists) developed a similar finding to the 2009 study by Francis, Gubb and Robbins noted above. In the sample of 148 male ministers, 15 of the 16 types were represented – all bar ESFP – and in the sample of female ministers only 13 of the 16 types – no representatives of ISTP, ISFP or ENTJ. The profile of Free Church ministers was found to be 'much closer to the profile of Anglican clergy than to the profile of the population as a whole'.[21] In respect of the profile of Anglican clergy, the study observed that

> The most startling difference between the psychological type profile of Church of England clergy and the general population occurs in respect of the Perceiving process. While 27% of men at large prefer iNtuition, the proportion rises to 62% among Church of England clergymen. While 21% of women at large prefer iNtuition, the proportion rises to 65% among Church of England clergywomen. Once again, however, the difference between clergymen and clergywomen is small.[22]

The 2011 study of women priests in the Church of England by Leslie Francis, Mandy Robbins and Michael Whinney[23] sought to replicate the 2007 study by Francis, Craig, Whinney, Tilley and Slater. In the new sample of 83 clergywomen serving in the Church of England diocese in the West Midlands, 14 of the 16 types were represented, ESFP and ENTJ both being absent. The study found that the results did replicate those of the earlier study, with clergywomen reporting preferences signifi-cantly differing from the UK population norms provided by Kendall[24] – for the Perceiving function of iNtuition (60 per cent compared with 21 per cent) and the orientation of Introversion (63 per cent compared with 43 per cent). In considering the implications of these results for the exercise of Christian ministry, the first was that the iNtuition preference would tend to focus ministry on the visionary rather than the practical, and the Introversion preference on the inward, prayerful path rather than the outward, social path. The second was that the disparities between the psychological profiles of clergywomen and the female population at large might lead to the former being regarded as 'impractical day-dreamers' and 'withdrawn, unsociable, difficult to get to know'.[25] The study sounded a caveat that its conclusions are limited by such a relatively small sample size.

One very interesting recent study is a psychological profile of Church of England bishops.[26] Leslie Francis, Michael Whinney and Mandy Robbins set up a study to examine what the Church of England requires of bishops and to see how the people match up to that requirement. The 1662 Ordinal in the Book of Common Prayer for the consecration of bishops sets out three requirements of the office of bishop. They are to

- instruct the people;
- banish and drive away from the Church all erroneous and strange doctrine;
- maintain and set forward . . . Quietness, love, and peace among all men; and such as be un-quiet, disobedient, and criminals, within your diocese, correct and punish.[27]

Mapping those requirements on to the psychological type model, the following preferences would be required: Sensing,

Thinking and Judging – an STJ profile. This type would typically provide 'a tight management structure in which precision is more important than vision, systems more important than people, and structure more important than flexibility'.[28]

The revised Ordinal in *Common Worship*[29] goes into more detail that reinforces the requirement for the STJ profile, but there is an added emphasis on the office being of an outgoing nature; this would tend to indicate a desired profile of ESTJ. The study of bishops compared the results of its own research with those from two studies previously described, the one in 2007 publishing a profile on 626 Church of England clergymen, and in 2010 a profile on another group of 622 clergy, in which two studies the profiles were strikingly similar.

One of the findings of the comparison made between the type profiles of clergy and bishops was that the EST profile designed for bishops is markedly dissimilar to that of the majority of clergy who have an INF profile. It is only in the Judging preference that the desired bishops' profile reflects the pool of those clergy from which they will be selected.

This 2013 study by Francis, Whinney and Robbins was responded to by 168 of the 258 bishops polled. The conclusions reached by the study were threefold.

1 The ability of psychological type theory to highlight those psychological characteristics associated with diocesan bishops. Their preferences are typically ESTJ, whose profile describes an individual good at managing systems and at safeguarding traditions and structures. They will typically not be as good at handling people, envisioning innovative developments or embracing change. They will be guardians of the tradition rather than visionary leaders.

2 How the study has illuminated the difference in psychological type between suffragan bishops and diocesan bishops:

'The main difference is between appointing the system-centred head to the diocesan post, and the person-centred heart to the suffragan post.'[30]

3 A suggestion that the Church of England should be invited to consider applying psychological type theory routinely within its human resource strategy, not only to make certain aspects of selecting people more transparent but also with a clear view of those characteristics needed for effective ministry and mission at the different levels of structure. The Church would do well to use a psychological assessment in aiding selection process.

The article ends with a question: 'As the Church of England selects the next generation of diocesan bishops, will the church be best served by continuing to place confidence in the STJ profile, with its strong emphasis on preserving the traditions of the organization?'[31] A conjecture is then put forward:

> Might the church be better served (in some dioceses at least) by, say, the ENFP profile of bishops who are equipped to function confidently with public visibility, to shape the vision for the future, to motivate the hearts of men and women to catch that vision, and to respond to the changing contours of a mission led church?[32]

The caveat would be that such a profile of bishop would need to be supported and complemented by an ISTJ–ESTJ team to maintain the essential diocesan infrastructure.

What we have looked at so far has illustrated that the developing body of research into the personality type profiles of those engaged in Christian ministry has tended to focus on establishing the type profiles of a number of different groupings. Research studies have been conducted on religious leadership and on the psychological type of a variety of church workers and leaders, both in training and in post.

The focus of most of the research conducted thus far has been on establishing the type profiles of each of these groupings. It has found that similar preferences have been expressed by Anglican clergymen and clergywomen, both genders expressing preferences for Introversion, Feeling and Judging. Roman Catholic priests in the UK share the same preferences. There is a difference in the preferences for the Perceiving process between Anglican clergy serving in England, where the preference is for iNtuition, and those serving in Wales, where the preference is for Sensing. Roman Catholic priests in the UK report nearly equal preferences for Sensing and iNtuition. Free Church ministers (Methodists and Baptists) also report preferences for Introversion, iNtuition, Feeling and Judging.

A different picture emerges of the evangelical wing of the Church. Church leaders on a Spring Harvest course, Lead Elders in the Newfrontiers network, Assemblies of God Bible college students, missionaries in training, seminarians and Bible college students in England all report preferences for Sensing and Judging, and predominant preferences for Extraversion and Thinking. The one exception is the male lay leaders in the 2005 study by Francis, Craig, Horsfall and Ross noted above,[33] who reported a preference for iNtuition.

So we can see from these studies that there is a variety of psychological types to be found among the people exercising Christian ministry. Collating the data, it can be seen that the predominant types reported among Anglican and Free Church clergy represented eight of the 16 types – ISTJ (three occurrences), ISFJ (six), INFJ (two), INTJ (four), INFP (three), ENFP (two), ESFJ (two) and ENFJ (two). Of these 24 occurrences, 15 expressed an IJ preference and nine an NF preference. Two-thirds of the preferences were for Introversion (18 compared with six). Of the 20 predominant types reported by evangelicals, only five of the 16 types were reported – ISTJ (seven occurrences), ISFJ (four), INFP (one), ESTJ (three), ESFJ (five) – with 60 per cent of the preferences being for Introversion (12 compared with eight).

In reviewing the body of research applying psychological type theory to Christian leadership, the 2009 study by Francis, Gubb and Robbins noted above observed that

> two main conclusions emerge . . . that there are some fairly consistent differences between the psychological type profiles of church leaders across denominations and the psychological type profile of the United Kingdom population as a whole; and that there are some significant differences in the psychological type profile of church leaders from different denominational, theological or ecclesial backgrounds.[34]

In the interests of academic rigour, I just need to sound a note of caution in that a number of the studies conducted in this field have used MBTI Form G (Anglicized) while the normative data for the UK population were generated using its successor, MBTI Step I. Further research is needed to substantiate earlier findings.

Only two of these studies begin to address the implications of the type preferences expressed in terms of the exercise of Christian ministry, namely the 2007 study by Francis, Craig, Whinney, Tilley and Slater[35] and the one in 2010 by Francis, Robbins, Duncan and Whinney.[36] Only one, Francis and Payne,[37] addressed the issue of ministry styles associated with type preferences.

Having reviewed all this research profiling clergy using the MBTI, it is apparent that there are people of each of the 16 Myers-Briggs® types undertaking, or preparing for, Christian ministry. I could therefore see the need for further research that applied personality type theory, type by type, to a model of Christian ministry in order to provide a 'guidebook' for ministers and those with whom they work, especially in managing those aspects of the exercise of their calling that cause stress. The overarching purpose would be to help Christian ministers better understand themselves in the day-to-day practice of, and development in, their ministry. I hope and trust that this book will serve that purpose.

Discerning the influence of type on Christian leaders

———•◆•———

Having identified the need for a set of type profiles as a 'guidebook' for ministers and those with whom they work, I discovered that developing a final shape for the profile was an iterative process. I chose a sample type and started to draft the profile. It became very clear, very quickly, that writing a type profile in the style of an academic paper, with its formal style and multiple referencing, would not provide the useful, and usable, format I had envisaged. I decided that the type profile should take a more discursive style, synthesizing various component elements – published research papers, the extensive literature on the MBTI®, insights drawn from practitioner training and courses attended, and personal experience as a parish priest, as an MBTI practitioner working with clergy and other Christian ministers, not least in jointly running personality and prayer workshops at Lee Abbey (among other places), and as a spiritual director using MBTI in the practice of direction.

In preparation for the drafting enterprise, I undertook a substantial amount of reading, both of academic papers and published literature. I had already qualified as a registered practitioner of Myers-Briggs® Step I and Step II at Emmaus House in Bristol, taught by the incomparable Ann O'Sullivan, who was instrumental in bringing the MBTI to the UK in 1980. I attended three additional courses there, also led by Ann – Type and Leadership, MBTI and Type Dynamics, and MBTI and Teams. A key element of the type profile that I identified was the application of type dynamics – Jung's function-attitudes – to each aspect of Christian ministry. I will go into this in more detail at the start of Part Two.

The overall shape of the type profile evolved into the following elements:

- an introduction that includes a heading in Jungian terminology; for example, Introverted iNtuition with Extraverted Thinking, a 'thumbnail sketch' of the type and a description of the characteristics of the type, including that type's approach to decision-making;
- a section on those aspects of Christian ministry that fall within that type's 'comfort zone';
- a section on those aspects that are 'outside comfort zone';
- a section on the type's response to stress, including what being in the 'grip' of the 'inferior function' would look like and how the type might approach getting out of it;
- a section setting out some strategies for reducing stress levels;
- a final summary to complement the thumbnail sketch at the beginning.

In order for the type profile to be the useful tool envisaged, it was necessary to develop a model of Christian ministry against which the function-attitudes of each type could be mapped.

The core of the type profile would be the model of ministry against which the various functions would be analysed. Different models of ministry have been developed over the years, some basing their analysis on ministry roles, others on ministry functions. Where role was the focus, researchers identified:

- Blizzard: six roles;[1]
- Nelsen, Yokley and Madron, five;[2] as did Reilly;[3]
- Tiller made it eight;[4]
- Lauer expanded the list to ten;[5]
- Francis and Rodger went back to seven;[6]
- Robbins and Francis expanded the list to ten.[7]

A functional approach was taken by both Davies, Watkins and Winter, who identified eight functions,[8] and Ranson, Bryman and Hinings, who identified seven.[9] I have tabulated the results so that you can see the overlap between these different approaches, and have included the model I developed to show both the overlap and my additions (see Table 4, overleaf).

Payne based his analysis of individual differences among clergy on Jungian psychology as put into usable form by the MBTI.[10] He moved away from the idea of ministry roles towards the idea of ministry styles. He used ten statements that described each of the eight Jungian functions of extraversion, introversion, sensing, intuition, thinking, feeling, judging and perceiving. These were refined down to seven statements by Francis and Payne.[11] So for the INTJ type, the statements below were relevant.

Introversion

- Refreshed by spending time alone in prayer.
- Gain energy conducting worship with small groups.
- Energized by giving time to preparing sermons.
- Refreshed by reading about a theological topic in depth.
- Energized by reading and writing in the study.
- Energized by contemplative prayer.
- Vitalized by praying for people.

iNtuition

- Enjoy discovering the gospel truth afresh in our own day.
- When preaching, like to leave people with questions.
- Like to think up new ways of doing things in the parish.
- Having a vision for the future is rewarding in my ministry.
- Enjoy raising questions of faith that others find difficult to answer.
- Like to question religious traditions whenever possible.
- Like finding solutions to new problems of faith.

Table 4 Ministry models

Role/Function	Blizzard	Nelsen et al.	Reilly	Tiller	Lauer	Francis and Rodger	Robbins and Francis	Davies et al.	Ranson et al.	Osborne
Teacher/Christian education	✓	✓	✓		✓		✓			
Organizer	✓		✓		✓					
Preacher	✓				✓		✓		✓	
Administration	✓	✓	✓		✓	✓	✓	✓	✓	✓
Pastor/visitor	✓		✓	✓	✓	✓	✓	✓	✓	✓
Priest/priest-ritual celebrant of sacraments	✓		✓			✓	✓	✓	✓	
Traditional		✓								
Counselling/counsellor		✓			✓	✓	✓		✓	
Community problem-solving		✓								
Prophet			✓						✓	
Leader				✓						
Focus of community/community leader				✓		✓	✓			
Public spokesman/official/representative				✓					✓	
Guardian of the tradition				✓						
Professional minister				✓						

Enabler of laity	✓					
Church builder	✓					
Prayer and worship/leader of public worship			✓			✓ ✓
Care and comfort		✓		✓		
Evangelism and mission/evangelist		✓		✓		
Stewardship and finance		✓				
Fellowship and service		✓				
Publicity and promotion		✓				
Public relations		✓				
Spiritual director				✓		
Private devotions and study					✓	
Diocesan and deanery duties					✓	
Travelling between events					✓	
Other duties					✓	
Church fabric						✓
Running meetings						✓
Visioning						✓
Occasional offices						✓
Social action						✓

Thinking

- Dealings with parishioners – pursue what is fair and just.
- Usually objective in pastoral crises.
- More important in ministry to be effective than liked.
- Logical analysis helps in parish life.
- Taking tough decisions in the parish is not difficult.
- Rewarding to settle disputes with parishioners objectively.
- Try to explore the logical consequences of actions.

Judging

- Like to plan down to the last detail in parish work.
- Any changes in the parish should be carefully planned.
- Like services to be well thought out in advance.
- Prefer to run parish according to a strict schedule.
- Think things should be kept in order in church.
- Good leadership involves good planning in church.
- Usually list things that need to be done each day in parish.

Following an analysis of these statements and the roles and functions identified by the studies detailed above, I developed my own model of ministry for my research that defined Christian ministry into nine categories:

1 worship
2 prayer
3 administration
4 pastoral care
5 church fabric
6 running meetings
7 visioning
8 occasional offices
9 social action.

This model was then used for the subsequent analysis included in the type profiles by creating a matrix with, on one axis, the type dynamics function-attitudes:

- Dominant
- Auxiliary
- Tertiary
- Inferior.

On the other axis were the above nine categories of the ministry model. The matrix was then annotated with characteristics of each type. For how an example type looked, see Table 5, overleaf ('JDI' stands for 'just do it').

This tabulation helped me to identify those categories that the MBTI theory would suggest would be in the type's comfort zone and those that would not. In drafting the prose descriptions for a given type, I kept referring to the annotated matrix for that type and applied not only my personal knowledge and experience of what is involved in a given element of the model of ministry, but also personal experience of individuals of that type in ministry. So, for example, ISFP vicars or curates approaching church fabric will be observant of details and appreciative of the aesthetic qualities of a church building using their Auxiliary Extraverted Sensing function. However, given their Dominant Introverted Feeling function, their interest in the fabric is only likely to be kindled if there is some emotional significance, some resonance with their internal value system or a link with past people who are significant to the ISFP.

In developing the thumbnail sketch and introduction sections, the type descriptions developed by Isabel Briggs Myers,[12] Jenny Rogers[13] and Malcolm Goldsmith and Martin Wharton[14] were particularly helpful, as were the insights into Jungian typology and the Myers-Briggs type developed by Angelo Spoto.[15]

The styles exhibited by types in a work environment were gathered from Otto Kroeger and Janet Thuesen,[16] Jean Kummerow, Nancy Barger and Linda Kirby,[17] Roger Pearman and Sarah Albritton[18] and Rowan Bayne.[19] These also informed the descriptions

Table 5 Sample matrix showing ministry model correlated with type dynamics

The ISFP type

	Worship	Prayer	Admin	Pastoral care	Fabric	Running meetings	Visioning	Occasional offices	Social action
Dominant Introverted Feeling	Passion Intensity	Alone/small groups Silence People focus	If it matters to them	Tolerant Accepting Good listeners Genuine desire to help Value people Non-judgemental	Link with past people Emotional significance?	Only if they matter		Need to help	Values Force for social change
Auxiliary Extraverted Sensing	Creative Artistic Practical suggestions	Tactile JDI	Good at practical details		Aesthetic appreciation Observant		No!	Practical help	Recognize opportunity Here and now
Tertiary iNtuition									
Inferior Extraverted Thinking									

of a type's leadership style, as did Lee and Norma Barr,[20] Jenny Rogers again,[21] Leslie Francis[22] and notes from the Type and Leadership course at Emmaus House, Bristol.

Insights about how a type would be likely to work in teams were gleaned from Rowan Bayne, Jenny Rogers, Elizabeth Hirsh, Katherine Hirsh and Sandra Krebs Hirsh,[23] and notes from The MBTI and Team Building and Team Work course at Emmaus House.

In starting to apply the MBTI® to the model of ministry used for this study, I grew to understand the paramount importance of type dynamics. As the MBTI user's guide states:

> The MBTI® instrument is one of the few personality questionnaires to be based on a comprehensive and psychodynamic theory of personality. The four MBTI® dichotomies are not independent dimensions, but form a dynamic whole, each part interacting with each other part, rather like the elements in a chemical compound.[24]

The descriptions of, and insights into, the workings of the inferior function developed by Henry Thompson,[25] Katharine Myers and Linda Kirby[26] and Naomi Quenk[27] were mined, together with notes from the MBTI and Type Dynamics course at Emmaus House.

Where aspects of prayer and spirituality were considered, personal experience as an MBTI practitioner, a rural dean and a spiritual director was augmented by the work of Charles Keating,[28] Bruce Duncan,[29] Ruth Fowke[30] and Julia McGuinness.[31]

Turning to how types would tend to respond to stress, what it would be like if the stress were to become overwhelming (being in the grip of the inferior function), possible routes out of the 'grip' experience, and strategies for avoiding or reducing the impact of stressful activities, the work of Naomi Quenk and Katharine Myers and Linda Kirby was again very informative, as again were notes from the MBTI and Type Dynamics course. The summary section then returned to Isabel Briggs Myers, Jenny Rogers and Malcolm Goldsmith and Martin Wharton as reference material.

So having read a multitude of books and research papers, analysed and distilled their wisdom, done some concentrated thinking and come up with a framework that would allow me to develop pen-portraits of the 16 different psychological types engaged in Christian ministry, I set about writing them. This was the basis for Part Two of this book, to which we now turn.

Part 2

16 TYPES OF
CHRISTIAN LEADER

Introduction to the type profiles

A lot has been written about the Myers-Briggs Type Indicator®
(MBTI®) – not, as some corporate subjects might privately
think, 'More B****y Therapeutic Interference'.

The MBTI has been developed over a number of decades,
from Carl Gustav Jung's thinking about human typology into
one of the foremost psychometric instruments in the world. It
is extensively used in personal and corporate development, in
building teams and in helping people to enrich their prayer lives.

This is not the place to go into the MBTI in great detail;
there are hundreds of books you can refer to if you want more
detailed analysis, and a number of registered practitioners who
would be delighted to help. Suffice to say that the MBTI is not
about IQ, ability or learned skills. It is about how a person
prefers to interact with the world.

A brief canter through the theory, then.

In Jungian typology, and in the MBTI that operationalizes
it, we humans embody an energy system that constantly takes
in information, from both the outside world and from inside
ourselves, evaluates and processes it and makes decisions. This
energy system is made up of pairs of possible preferences in
four areas:

1 where we prefer to draw our emotional energy – external or
internal;
2 how we prefer to acquire information – facts or hunches;
3 how we prefer to process that information and come to a
decision – head or heart;
4 what we prefer to do with the processed result – closure or
open-ended.

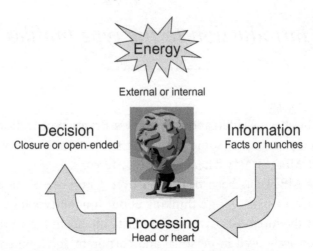

Figure 3 The four preference pairs in diagrammatic form

Figure 3 offers a diagrammatic expression of this.

In the same way that one is normally a natural right- or left-hander – preferring to use one hand over the other, and doing so with more facility – so the MBTI preferences are just that: preferences. It is not that one cannot use any of the eight preferences, one just prefers to use one of each pair because it feels more comfortable, more natural.

When the MBTI discernment process has been undertaken, the resulting preferences are designated by four letters, one for each preference. The MBTI preference pairs are shown in Table 6.

Table 6 The four preference pairs in text form with their letter designations

Energy	Extraversion	Introversion
Information	Sensing	iNtuition
Processing	Thinking	Feeling
Decision	Judging	Perceiving

The terms are Jung's and have the very specific meaning he gave them in his typology. Most of us will immediately think that an Extravert is one who is the life and soul of the party and an Introvert one who is shy and retiring. Not so in the MBTI. Either type can exhibit behaviours more 'typical' of the other. It is just that, typically, the Extravert will gain energy from being with people, the Introvert will find it draining, and vice versa.

The E–I axis

One quick way to check your preference on the E–I axis is to think what you would do if you were feeling emotionally drained. Would your instinct be to seek out another person, perhaps even go to a party, or would it be to curl up alone with a book or the TV? Extraverts will typically do the first, Introverts the second. Similarly with the three other pairs.

The S–N axis

Instinctively one will prefer to acquire information either through the senses – facts and figures, hard data – or by using some sixth sense to 'hear the music, not just the words'. A quick way to check your preference on this axis is to look at a picture for 20 seconds and then describe the picture to somebody. If you remember the details, what was where, how many, what colour and so on, chances are that you are a Sensor. If you remember the mood of the picture, what it might mean, how it made you feel, chances are you are an iNtuitor.

The T–F axis

Once the information has been acquired, the preference may be for thinking through the situation, logically and objectively or for working out how personal needs and feelings – your own and others' – might be affected. Again a quick check: if you have a situation to deal with, do you stand outside the issue and objectively work out a solution, or do you put yourself inside the situation and work out how it makes you feel? A Thinker will typically do the first, a Feeler the second.

The J–P axis

This axis indicates one's attitude to the world. Is the preference for coming to a decision or for going with the flow? Having processed the information you have acquired, the preference will be either to leave things fluid – to see what else may turn up – or to seek closure, to have things done and dusted. The Judging preference will always seek closure, the Perceiving preference open-endedness. Again, a diagram may help (see Figure 4).

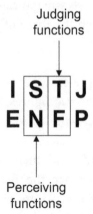

Figure 4 **The Perceiving and Judging functions**

Thus the result of taking the MBTI psychometric test will be a four-letter series, such as ESTJ or INFP, indicating the preferences the testee has reported. A profile of the type indicated is then talked through with the practitioner who has administered the test.

It has been said that the MBTI is a great tool but an appalling weapon. It would be incorrect to view it as a 'box' into which individuals can be categorized. It is much more helpful to view the MBTI as a 'growbag' that provides a base from which one can grow and develop – or a 16-roomed house in which one is most at ease in one particular room.

The important thing is that one lives with the resulting type profile for a while to see if it feels comfortable. It is possible that the 'fit' does not feel entirely right. There is a more detailed test – MBTI Step II – that goes into greater depth. This was my own personal experience. I had completed the Step I questionnaire on three occasions and come out as a type that did not quite fit. I then took the Step II test, and found that the 'F' preference was actually a 'T' – I was a much better fit with the resulting profile.

More theory

Where it gets even more interesting is that the four functions in the resulting type – Sensing or iNtuiting and Thinking or Feeling – are used in a given order. This may happen in a matter of seconds, and typically unconsciously, but it still happens. So as noted in the previous chapter, in the order in which they are used there is

1 a Dominant function
2 an Auxiliary function
3 a Tertiary function
4 an Inferior function.

As we have seen, an MBTI is expressed as four letters, for example, ESTJ. The two 'outside' preferences (in this case 'E' and 'J') signify the orientation preference that is either towards the outer world or the inner world – Extraversion–Introversion – and what Jung termed the 'attitude' preference that is either towards closure and completion or towards open-endedness and 'going with the flow'– Judging–Perceiving. The order in which one uses the four functions – the 'inside' pair of either

Sensing or iNtuition and Thinking or Feeling – depends on those two 'outside' preferences.

The two pairs of 'inside' preferences (what Jung termed 'functions') are the Perceiving functions (Sensing or iNtuiting) and the Judging functions (Thinking and Feeling). So if you have a preference for 'Judging' (your last letter is J), for example ESTJ, your Dominant will be Thinking, because that is your Judging function. Which one is the Dominant function depends on the first preference – Extraverts will be happy for the world to see the best of themselves so their Judging function of Thinking will be their Dominant. It will be the first function to be used in assessing any situation – and it will be the first impression others will get of the person: cerebral, objective, analytical. Diagrammatically, this is shown in Figure 5.

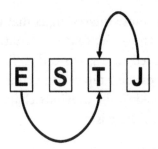

Figure 5 The fourth preference (J or P) points to what the world sees, the first preference (E or I) points to the Dominant for an E

Where the preference is for Introversion, on the other hand, for example ISTJ, the individual will want to hide their best from public view, so the world will still see their Judging function of Thinking but it will be their Auxiliary function. Their Dominant function will be Sensing, so it will be the first function to be used in assessing a situation (the need for hard facts and the details), while the first impression others will get of the person will still be from the Extraverted Thinking (cerebral, objective, analytical). Again, diagrammatically this is shown in Figure 6.

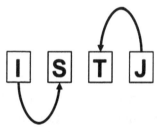

Figure 6 The fourth preference (J or P) points to what the world sees, the first preference (E or I) points to the Dominant for an I

The circle of usage then follows in order – the Auxiliary will be the first of the opposite pair, the Tertiary will be its counterpart, then the Inferior will be the opposite of the Dominant. The same circle is followed, whichever is the Dominant, so wherever you start, be it S, N, T or F, the order in which the functions are used – the type dynamics – always go Judging to Perceiving to Perceiving to Judging or Perceiving to Judging to Judging to Perceiving (see Figure 7).

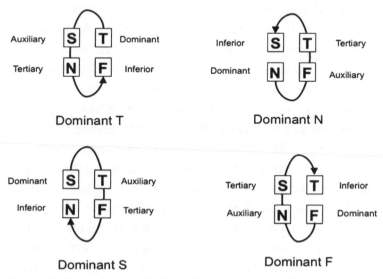

Figure 7 The order in which the functions are used

Into the shadows

So one's 'preferred function' is the Dominant/Auxiliary pair –
ST, SF, NF or NT. Jung had little to say about the Tertiary
function, but the Inferior function – sometimes inaccurately
termed the Shadow function – is where life can get really
interesting. It is the Inferior function that triggers when we
are stressed. It is the Inferior function that makes us behave
atypically. But it is also the Inferior function where one can
have the most profound prayer experiences.

To put it another way, type dynamics are concerned with the
four functions: Sensing, iNtuition, Thinking and Feeling. An
individual has a preference for making more use of two of the
four functions (their Dominant and Auxiliary functions). The
Dominant function is determined by both the orientation and
the attitude of the type. The attitude – Judging or Perceiving –
will indicate which function is visible to the outside world.
So an individual with a Judging preference will display his or
her Judging function – Thinking or Feeling – to the world
at large. The individual's orientation will determine whether
that function is the Dominant or the Auxiliary. An individual
with an Extraversion orientation will be content for his or her
best to be on show, so that function will be the Dominant;
for an individual with an Introversion preference, it will be
the Auxiliary function. The Tertiary and Inferior functions
are the opposite function of the Dominant–Auxiliary pair – the
Inferior opposite the Dominant and the Tertiary opposite
the Auxiliary. The four functions are used in a specified order,
particularly in decision-making – first the Dominant, then the
Auxiliary, then the Tertiary and finally the Inferior. Using
the analogy of a car, the Dominant is the driver, the Auxiliary
is the map-reader in the passenger seat, the Tertiary is the
teenager in the seat behind the map-reader and the Inferior is
the baby asleep in the car-seat behind the driver.

This becomes important when there is a lot of stress about. The Inferior function will tend to kick in when someone is stressed – the baby suddenly wakes up and yells, probably causing a bit of a wobble in the car analogy. If and when a period of stress is prolonged, and indeed becomes the normal state of affairs, there is a tendency for the Dominant and Inferior functions to 'flip' – a state known as being in the grip of the Inferior function. Atypical behaviours result, sometimes with disastrous results. In the car analogy, the baby reaches over the front seat, grabs the steering-wheel and says 'Now I'm driving!' Not a state of affairs to be desired.

Jung's typology states that we tend to spend the first half of our lives specializing in, and developing, our preferred function – ST, SF, NF or NT. Once we reach the second half of life – at age 35 or so – we have the choice of staying with that specialization or beginning to integrate our less preferred functions. If we choose to stay with our specialization, the tendency will be for us to become rather inflexible stereotypes of that function and fail to take advantage of the richness of integration. If we become more comfortable with our less preferred functions, we need less emotional energy to use them and are on the road to the fullness of who we were born to be.

In the following type profiles, I have followed the usual con-vention in the MBTI world of setting out the four ST types first, followed by the SF types, then the NF types and finally the NT types. These are normally illustrated in a 4 × 4 table with the four columns set out in this order. OPP has developed really helpful summaries of each type, which they call 'Typies' (see Figure 8, overleaf).

If you visit OPP's website at <www.opp.com/en/Using-Type/MBTI-Step-I-Typies?src=hpcar> you will see that the Typies are all colour-coded, with each box outlined in the colour of

TYPIES STEP I

Competent Productive Theoretical
Innovative Independent Logical
INTJ
CONCEPTUAL PLANNER
Strategic Reflective Conceptual
Objective Insightful Demanding

Conceptual Analytical Innovative
Theoretical Detached Sceptical
INTP
OBJECTIVE ANALYST
Independent Challenging Logical
Strategic Insightful Contained

Compassionate Idealistic Intense
Visionary Imaginative Reflective
INFJ
INSIGHTFUL VISIONARY
Insightful Caring Contemplative
Reserved Empathetic Sensitive

Reflective Idealistic Spontaneous
Flexible Insightful Developmental
INFP
THOUGHTFUL IDEALIST
Compassionate Caring Imaginative
Complex Empathetic Contained

Considerate Sensitive Thorough
Dependable Responsible Loyal
ISFJ
PRACTICAL HELPER
Organised Practical Detailed Kind
Patient Realistic Understanding

Modest Adaptable Gentle Loyal
Practical Caring Accommodating
ISFP
VERSATILE SUPPORTER
Cooperative Observant Tolerant
Kind Considerate Spontaneous

Detached Analytical Observant
Thorough Conscientious Realistic
ISTJ
RESPONSIBLE REALIST
Practical Logical Factual Efficient
Systematic Organised Reserved

Adaptable Logical Independent
Realistic Trouble-shooter Factual
ISTP
LOGICAL PRAGMATIST
Analytical Emergent Practical
Expedient Detached Objective

Figure 8 OPP's Typies

Table 7 Type table with the Dominant function highlighted

I**S**TJ	I**S**FJ	I**N**FJ	I**N**TJ
Dominant Introverted Sensing with Extraverted Thinking	Dominant Introverted Sensing with Extraverted Feeling	Dominant Introverted iNtuition with Extraverted Feeling	Dominant Introverted iNtuition with Extraverted Thinking
IS**T**P	IS**F**P	IN**F**P	IN**T**P
Dominant Introverted Thinking with Extraverted Sensing	Dominant Introverted Feeling with Extraverted Sensing	Dominant Introverted Feeling with Extraverted iNtuition	Dominant Introverted Thinking with Extraverted iNtuition
ES**T**P	ES**F**P	EN**F**P	EN**T**P
Dominant Extraverted Sensing with Introverted Thinking	Dominant Extraverted Sensing with Introverted Feeling	Dominant Extraverted iNtuition with Introverted Feeling	Dominant Extraverted iNtuition with Introverted Thinking
ES**T**J	ES**F**J	EN**F**J	EN**T**J
Dominant Extraverted Thinking with Introverted Sensing	Dominant Extraverted Feeling with Introverted Sensing	Dominant Extraverted Feeling with Introverted iNtuition	Dominant Extraverted Thinking with Introverted iNtuition

the Dominant function – green for Sensing, red for Feeling, blue for Thinking and Yellow for iNtuition – and the type word pairs are the ones I have used in the type profiles. For the sake of completeness, Table 7 presents a simplified table with the Dominant highlighted.

1

Introducing the ISTJ leader – the Responsible Realist

Dominant Introverted Sensing with Extraverted Thinking

———•◦•———

ISTJs are characterized by their thoughtfulness, their need to assume responsibility and be in charge, and by their tendency to perfectionism. The overriding goal of ISTJs is to understand the world around them and their place in it. They will use their five senses to form an understanding that is solid, substantial and accurate.

* * *

Introduction

ISTJs focus on what they can see, hear, smell, touch and taste – on what is real and actual. They value practicality – practical applications, facts, concrete things in the real world. They observe and remember sensory data; indeed, for things that are important to them they have an almost photographic memory and almost perfect recall of details. They are orientated to the present and they trust past experience; they distrust intuitive insights that seem to have no basis in reality.

ISTJs are typically very deep people and their lives are more about past memory than about present perception. Combined with their Introverted Sensing function, their Extraverted Thinking function helps them to organize things to get the job done – now! – and to get the job done, for now. ISTJs are highly task orientated and consider the reason for having other people around is that they are also there to do the job.

The type dynamics of the ISTJ show that the Dominant function is Introverted Sensing, the Auxiliary function is Extraverted Thinking, the Tertiary function is Introverted Feeling and the Inferior function is Extraverted iNtuition. ISTJs' Dominant Introverted Sensing function leads them to trust and rely on their internal database of actual events and realities. Their Auxiliary Extraverted Thinking function helps them to organize the external world, imposing structure and logically developed systems. The Tertiary function takes account of the impact any decisions they take may have on others and their value systems. Finally the Inferior Extraverted iNtuitive function expands the ISTJ's horizon to look at the big picture, making connections on a wider canvas and considering possibilities rather than actualities.

The four functions are used in four steps, one after the other – Dominant, Auxiliary, Tertiary and Inferior – but it is an unconscious, and very fast, process. The Tertiary and Inferior functions may be used minimally or not at all. If used, they may be less well executed, or even omitted altogether, if they have undergone little or no development. When confronted with a new situation, then, ISTJs' initial response will be to collect as much data as possible using their five senses, and referencing their internal database to see if there is any previous experience that can be brought to bear (Sensing). Having gathered the data, they will then apply logic to the situation to develop a rational response to the data gathered (Thinking). That response will then be reviewed in the light of the impact the response will have on others and their value systems (Feeling) and, finally, the ISTJ will look at the big picture – to see this situation in a wider context (iNtuition).

In a team environment, the contribution made by ISTJs is to classify information so that it is explicit and understandable. They will use logical argument that will be backed up by specific data and they will be rooted in reality. They may withhold their own view until the process has been going for some time, and they may be insensitive to the need for the 'softer' interpersonal skills.

ISTJs respect tradition, the status quo – 'Even if it is broke, let's not fix it; I like it as it is and always has been' – and are comfortable in organizational hierarchies. They can be inclined to be too serious, too rooted in routine, and typically will expect others to conform to standard operating procedures, thus stifling innovation.

As leaders ISTJs quietly get on with organizing and maintaining order by applying logic, reason and common sense. They will be good role models for efficiency and dependability.

Comfort zone

A preference for Introversion will incline the Introverted Sensor towards quiet forms of worship that allow inner reflection, while providing concrete, factual material to work on. The Thinking preference will mean that a cognitive process, working on the concrete details, within the context of a structured and controlled service form, will provide the most satisfactory worship experience.

ISTJs will lead worship competently and accurately, but will find unstructured worship forms uncomfortable. Being required to operate in an Extraverted way in leading worship will tend to be tiring and recovery time will be needed, especially if two or three services have been conducted in succession.

The Introverted pray-er is likely to prefer praying alone or in small groups. God is likely to be experienced as the 'still small voice' and as transcendent, unknowable and inaccessible.

Silence and solitude will be preferred; too much noise or action will be very distracting.

The preference for Sensing will typically involve a step-by-step approach to spiritual growth, and Sensors will prefer to be able to see details of their progress. They will typically enjoy routines in their prayer lives – a regular, structured prayer discipline like a Daily Office will be nourishing. Any changes to their prayer routine will need to be fully justified. God is experienced in the here and now, simply, undramatically, and often in the natural world. Often the Sensing pray-er will be helped by the use of something tangible – for example, music, a picture, rosary beads, incense.

As a Sensor Thinker, the Thinking aspects of prayer will also be nourishing; the Thinking pray-er will like structure and dislike repetition. Intelligibility will be important, as will the exercise of logic and reason. The search for truth and meaning will be a continual one, and God tends to be found in the mind and in experience. The doctrine of the Church to which the thinker belongs will be important. Bible study will actually become prayer in the classical Lectio Divina sense of reading and meditating on the word. Emotionalism in worship or prayer, or numinous religious experiences, will be thought suspect.

For the ISTJ the orderly prayer preferred by the Judging preference will fit well with the Sensing preference. Well-organized prayer and worship times, with a logical structure, will be preferred. Familiarity will be preferred over novelty, and the use of set liturgical forms of prayer will be comforting. Order, structure and discipline will be very important, not only as the form that carries them through times of barrenness but also as a stable base on which a more open style can be built.

The STJ preference will enjoy concentrating on tasks that need doing, and administration may be an enjoyable aspect of working life. Planning of parish work, a timetable to be followed and lists of things that need to be done each day will be characteristic.

As Sensor Thinkers, ISTJs will tend to preach from the head rather than from the heart. There will typically be a logical progression from point to point, coming to a well-reasoned conclusion. Sermons or talks will be informative rather than exciting but will always be well crafted. The intellectual satisfaction of preparing and delivering any form of teaching will be pleasing. Preaching to a large congregation or teaching large groups will tend to be tiring rather than energizing, but they will both be done with clarity and precision if not with charisma.

The Sensing preference gathers information using the five senses. An interest in the form and beauty of church buildings will lead the Sensor to be aware of the state of the church fabric. In the Anglican Church there is a five-yearly inspection (the quinquennial inspection) by the church architect that results in a report detailing the actions that need to be taken – repairs done, gutters cleared, lightning conductors inspected and operational – over the following five years. The inevitable process of applying for a Faculty from the Chancellor of the diocese will be meat and drink to the ISTJ, especially the complexity that Listed Building status brings. Ministers in other denominations where there is no such process may still have to negotiate the local authority planning process. The Sensor will tend to keep a keen eye on such issues. If the church needs to be decorated or if there is a re-ordering project, the Sensor will tend to be involved in, and nourished by, the fine detail.

The STJ preference will relish the order and structure of a well-run meeting. Standard operating procedures, standing instructions and the intricacies of meeting etiquette will be well in the comfort zone. Excursions from the agenda and lots of unstructured any other business will be found trying.

The STJ with an Introversion preference will find meetings tiring rather than energizing, especially if the meeting is a large one. One can be sure that the ISTJ will be very well prepared for any meeting he or she attends, and woe betide anybody who challenges a memory about something important to that individual. The near-photographic memory and almost perfect recall of the ISTJ will usually mean an uncanny level of accuracy.

The idea of doing something concrete to further the kingdom, especially something that has been proven to work somewhere else, will be attractive. Initiatives such as city mission projects, night shelters for the homeless, breakfast clubs for street people, or delivering gifts house by house to a street of homes, will appeal greatly. Again the Introversion preference will make such outwardly focused work tiring but it will nonetheless be deeply satisfying for the ISTJ.

Outside comfort zone

A preference for Introversion will make ad hoc pastoral visiting less than congenial. Visiting people, individuals or groups will be a duty rather than a pleasure. Meeting new people will be draining rather than energizing.

The ISTJ thinks carefully, rationally and logically and is able to spot logical flaws and inconsistencies very quickly. The development of a vision will not come naturally to the ISTJ as this tends to be the province of the intuitive thinker. If the ISTJ is in a leadership position, there will be a need to find trusted colleagues who think creatively and imaginatively. ISTJs will be very good at building on new ideas, provided they trust the person who has generated those ideas, using their knowledge and experience of what has worked before.

The conduct of preparatory meetings for baptisms, funerals and weddings will be efficient and will get the job done. There will tend to be a lack of natural warmth and a focus on the nuts and bolts of the services themselves rather than the emotional human issues that will be around. It is likely that the occasional offices will be done to the general satisfaction of the 'consumers' but the use of the less preferred Extraversion and Feeling functions will again be tiring.

Stress response

The Dominant function of the ISTJ is Introverted Sensing. Using their preferred perceiving function of Sensing in their inner world, ISTJs absorb sensory information and experiences, reflect on them and remember, in great detail, the things that are important to them. ISTJs trust their senses; they trust experience, both past and present, and feel uncomfortable moving beyond sensory experience until it is thoroughly understood.

ISTJs apply themselves to facts and details, carefully and in an orderly fashion, and distrust people who treat facts in a cavalier way and are sloppy about details. ISTJs are responsible, conscientious and dependable, and they value traditions, organizational hierarchies and institutions. They give every appearance of being well grounded in reality, being totally trustworthy, and they enjoy finding ways of being efficient and cost-effective by perfecting the tried and trusted techniques.

The ideal working environment for an ISTJ is one in which the focus is on facts and details, where the ISTJ can organize those facts and details in pursuit of the goal. ISTJs like to complete one thing before moving on to another, preferably working in their own dedicated space with few interruptions. They will be happiest with organizational structures with clear reporting lines and operating procedures, and where expectations are explicit. They will function best where they are in control of their own work schedule, where they have little or no time pressure and are in a supportive structure that allows them to perform to their own high standards.

Life becomes stressful when deadlines are imposed and pursued and when incomplete, inadequate or downright shoddy work done by others affects the quality of their own work. A sudden change, especially one that appears to have no good reason, will be anathema. If asked to do something inefficiently, ineffectively, imaginatively or by the seat of their pants, this will cause stress.

As stress levels increase, Introverted Sensing types use the Dominant function more and more. Their Auxiliary Thinking preference – the judging process – will typically be less and less used. Like a dog with a bone, the Introverted Sensor will focus on more and more details and more and more facts and become unable to discriminate between relevant and irrelevant information. This leads to a significant loss of effectiveness and the 'flip' between Dominant and Inferior functions occurs. The Inferior Extraverted iNtuition has little or no control over facts or details, produces impulsive behaviour and leads to catastrophizing – imagining all sorts of dire future possibilities.

When Introverted Sensors are in the grip of their Inferior function, negativity and pessimism predominate and there will be a see-saw between being open to the requests of others and withdrawal and resistance. Others will be blamed or accused of negativity, thoughtlessness or lack of caring; the usual efficiency and productivity of the Introverted Sensor will be absent and sleep will be hard to come by. There will usually be obsessive worrying at problems, sometimes fuelled by alcohol, until a state of stasis occurs. At this point the Introverted Sensor virtually shuts down, no work is done for extended periods, and then depression sets in.

It is highly unusual for a 'reverse flip' to occur, flipping back to the Introverted Sensing norm. The Tertiary function is very valuable in these circumstances. The Tertiary function of the ISTJ – Feeling – can help to assert the internal value system and the importance of group harmony. With the seeking of concrete and specific reassurance of their own worth, their competence and their track record can come a reduction in the negativity. Tackling small projects, with the down-to-earth support of others, completing them and meeting goals can reinforce that sense of self-worth.

Getting away from the work environment, spending time alone drinking in the sensory delights of creation can then be experienced as very healing.

Life-giving strategies

ISTJs will typically find it very hard to develop their Tertiary and Inferior functions. However, they will find that they become more effective if they can develop the ability to look at the big picture. If they can find an iNtuitive colleague whose opinion they trust, they may be able to make value judgements based on iNtuition, blue-sky thinking or just plain hunch rather than having to back them up with hard facts.

Developing a tolerance of ambiguity and refraining from demanding facts and figures to back up opinions may well be experienced as freeing. Any change to the existing order will often be perceived as threatening, so trying to seek out rather than crush creative, new ideas could be a positive experience and, when asked for an opinion, it will be helpful to 'accentuate the positive and eliminate the negative'.

There does not always have to be a decision immediately – learning to go with the flow might relieve pressure on self and others. It can also be very helpful to communicate feelings rather than having them guessed and probably got wrong. Widening the circle of social contact, especially moving out of the comfort zone of the 'usual suspects', can bring great benefits. A little gentle silliness and frivolity occasionally can work wonders.

Summary

The solemn, courteous, thoughtful, responsible, perfectionist ISTJ is rarely if ever off duty and may seem very intimidating. Leading by thorough and prudent planning, developing and implementing clear structures, targets, goals and systems, and by being hardworking and well organized, ISTJs will be respected for their work ethic and their memory for detail. They will, however, benefit from developing an ability to look at the big picture and learning to live with ambiguity.

2

Introducing the ISTP leader – the Logical Pragmatist

Dominant Introverted Thinking with Extraverted Sensing

———◆———

The overriding goal of an ISTP is to create logical order internally; to develop rational principles for understanding the world. They are always ready to analyse, use logic and cause-and-effect reasoning to solve problems, aspire to an impersonal, objective truth, are tough-minded, valuing fairness and seeking justice.

* * *

Introduction

ISTPs are troubleshooters who enjoy emergencies and pressure, solving practical problems flexibly and spontaneously. They are action-centred, focused in the present on the immediate situation, and prefer to work without the constraint of rules and regulations. While they enjoy variety, they can appear to be 'so laid-back as to be almost horizontal'.

The combination of reserve and being stimulated by 'fire-fighting' situations makes ISTPs something of an enigma and, indeed, they may enjoy making themselves hard to read. They do not enjoy routine, administration, checklists or any kind of restriction, and may appear indecisive or directionless. They tend towards abruptness and directness and may take shortcuts.

They get easily bored and need to be in a working environment where troubleshooting and response to emergencies is the norm.

ISTPs seek to bring order to their internal thoughts and develop a logical system for understanding them by Thinking through the information they have gathered with their five senses. They will seldom volunteer their thoughts and judgements but will do so if asked or if their logical analysis is challenged. As reflective observers, they process the information they have gathered, categorize it and develop a structure for understanding. They have high expectations of themselves, making and accepting no excuses.

Type dynamics show that the ISTP has a Dominant function of Introverted Thinking – absorbing and analysing precise data about the world around them. The Auxiliary function is Extraverted Sensing – homing in on the world's present, material realities. The Tertiary function of Introverted iNtuition looks for patterns in everyday events and the Inferior function of Extraverted Feeling considers the human dimension.

The four functions are used in four steps, one after the other – Dominant, Auxiliary, Tertiary and Inferior – but it is an unconscious, and very fast, process. The Tertiary and Inferior functions may be used minimally or not at all. If used, they may be less well executed, or even omitted altogether, if they have undergone little or no development. Faced with a new situation, then, the ISTP will instinctively begin to apply logic to the situation presenting (Thinking) before focusing on the facts and details (Sensing). In reality, of course, one cannot apply logic in the absence of any data, so if the ISTP's Judging function is Dominant, gathering data and processing it will be parallel activities. Once data has been gathered and logically analysed, the ISTP will review the situation and the rational solution in the light of the big picture, the wider world (iNtuition). Only then will the impact on others be considered (Feeling).

In a team environment, ISTPs contribute a precise and well-thought-out analysis of the present situation using the wide range of facts at their command. They can be overprecise and appear not to care by making no effort to share their own ideas. They will be put off by the more 'touchy-feely' members of the team who want to share feelings and want to locate a team within their own personal value system. Discussion that is not rooted in facts and appears to have no practical purpose will be irritating.

As leaders ISTPs are unobtrusive, realistic and even-handed, allowing a great degree of freedom that allows others to maximize the use of their own gifts and skills. Affirmation and praise will be rare and traditional hierarchical positions will be ignored. Getting the job done will be paramount so other team members who are not prepared to implement a 'quick and dirty' solution will be irksome. Conflicts within the team will be welcomed as an opportunity for problem-solving, which will be carried out with the ISTP's concrete grasp on details and on what is possible.

Comfort zone

The ideal working environment for a Dominant Introverted Thinker is one that gives ISTPs freedom to work in pursuit of their own interests and passions. The work will tend to be on concrete projects that can produce tangible results, and ISTPs will want to be free to work as many hours and as intensively as they want. They will want to be valued and respected for their own special expertise and have any contributions they make genuinely appreciated. While seeking autonomy and independence it will be important for the ISTP to be included and have his or her voice heard when matters of moment are being discussed and significant decisions made.

A preference for Introversion will incline the Sensor towards quiet forms of worship that allow inner reflection, while providing concrete, factual material to work on. The Thinking preference will mean that a cognitive process, working on the concrete details, within an open, less constrained context than that of a structured and controlled service form, will provide the most satisfactory worship experience as individuals with a Perceiving preference prefer worship to be flexible, with opportunities for going with the flow. Spontaneity and being open to the movement of the spirit will be important.

Being required to operate in an Extraverted way in leading worship will tend to be tiring and recovery time will be needed, especially if two or three services have been conducted in succession.

An individual with a preference for Introversion will be refreshed by spending time alone. Studying, reading and writing will be restorative, as will time given to the preparation of sermons. Researching a theological topic in depth will be congenial and attractive.

ISTPs have preferences for I, S, T and P, so as an Introverted pray-er, the ISTP is likely to prefer praying alone or in small groups. God is likely to be experienced as the 'still small voice' and as transcendent, unknowable and inaccessible. Silence and solitude will be preferred; too much noise or action will be very distracting.

The preference for Sensing will typically involve a step-by-step approach to spiritual growth, and Sensors will prefer to be able to see details of their progress. They will typically enjoy routines in their prayer lives – structured Daily Offices will be nourishing, such as those in the Franciscans' *Celebrating Common Prayer* or *Celtic Daily Prayer* from the Northumbria Community (see 'Further reading' at the back of this book). Any changes to their prayer routine will need to be fully justified. God is experienced in the here and now, simply, undramatically and often in the natural world. Often the Sensing pray-er will be helped by the use of something tangible – for example, music, a picture, rosary beads, incense.

The Thinking pray-er likes structure and dislikes repetition. Intelligibility will be important, as will the exercise of logic and reason. The search for truth and meaning will be a continual one, and God tends to be found in the mind and in experience. The doctrine of the church to which the thinker belongs will be important. Bible study will actually become prayer in the classical sense of reading and meditating on the word. Emotionalism in worship or prayer, or numinous religious experiences, will be thought suspect.

Perceiving pray-ers need to beware of the possibility that they may never settle down to a particular style of prayer. This can be confusing as they are the most open to different paths and types of spiritual growth. God is a God of possibilities, pleasure and fun. Typically individuals with a perceiving preference will find God in life through gathering experiences, insights, pleasures and relationships. They like to remain open to most possibilities and are comfortable with risk, ambiguity or an eclectic spirituality. They are happy to go with the flow and feel out of control, and may become rebellious or demotivated if faced with a restrictive routine. They can be intrigued by the infinite progression of the mystical tradition. To grow in their prayer lives, perceiving pray-ers need to retain their sense of freedom but to overlay it with a form of discipline. Great riches may be found in the Anglican Daily Office, for example.

Individuals with a preference for Sensing will want to focus on tasks that need doing in their parish ministry. God is the God of action, the God who saves, heals and triumphs. 'Call and response' will be very important. Action rather than reflection will be preferred, so the preference will be for doing things rather than Thinking about them. It may be that there is a call to a missionary context – daring to go out into the world and take action because God is calling. A religious order such as the Franciscans may offer the right mixture of freedom of action, a prayer discipline and a context for social action.

An individual with a preference for Sensing will find the process of administration congenial – keeping detailed accounts, completing diocesan returns, ensuring that electrical appliances have undergone annual PAT tests (electrical compliance tests) and fire extinguishers have been tested will all be grist to the Sensor's mill.

For individuals with a Thinking preference, the key measure in ministry will be effectiveness. Bringing objectivity to bear in crisis situations in ministry, the individual with the Thinking preference will pursue fairness and justice – being well liked will not be as important as finding a logical, reasoned solution. In taking difficult decisions in the church, rational analysis that explores possible courses of action and their logical consequences will be the norm. Reasoned settlement of disputes with members of the staff team or of the congregation will be pursued.

The rich variety of ministry with its unpredictable occurrences, new and unplanned experiences and the real possibility of a break in routine will be very attractive to those with a Perceiving preference.

Where a church or congregation has its own premises, church buildings will be important to an individual with a preference for Sensing. The five-yearly inspection of Anglican and Methodist Model Trust churches – the quinquennial inspection – and the subsequent report will be important to the Sensor. The list of tasks to be completed in the next five-year period may well be entered on a spreadsheet by the individual with a Sensing preference, and tasks scheduled and marked as completed.

Regular examination of the church fabric will be done with care to ensure that it is kept in order, and the individual with a Sensing preference will enjoy helping keep the building in good decorative order. If a re-ordering project is undertaken, the individual with a Sensing preference will be keen to be involved in the fine detail of the process. In the Anglican Church the process of obtaining a Faculty can be positively byzantine and the individual with a Sensing preference will relish the complexity and fine detail.

Outside comfort zone

A preference for Introversion will make ad hoc pastoral visiting less than congenial. Visiting people, individually or in groups, will be a duty rather than a pleasure. Meeting new people will be draining rather than energizing.

The ISTP thinks carefully, rationally and logically and is able to spot logical flaws and inconsistencies very quickly. The development of a vision will not come naturally to the ISTP as this tends to be the province of the iNtuitive thinker and the ISTP is firmly rooted in the present. If the ISTP is in a leadership position, there will be a need to find trusted colleagues who think creatively and imaginatively. ISTPs will be very good at building on new ideas, provided they trust those who have generated those ideas, using their knowledge and experience of what has worked before.

The conduct of preparatory meetings for baptisms, funerals and weddings will be efficient and will get the job done. There will tend to be a lack of natural warmth and a focus on the nuts and bolts of the services themselves rather than the emotional human issues that will be around. It is likely that the occasional offices will be done to the general satisfaction of the 'consumers' but the use of the less preferred Extraversion and Feeling functions will again be tiring.

Stress response

If the ISTP's working environment is one where he or she is under supervision and being required to work to strict rules and regulations, this will begin to be stressful. If that supervision is being done by somebody the ISTP views as incompetent, the stress will increase. If work colleagues are similarly incompetent, and especially if the ISTP is either responsible for or dependent on their work, this will only increase the feeling of stress. Illogicality, injustice or unfairness will all be stressors. If the working environment allows too little time for being alone, if the workspace is crowded or if the ISTP is required to work in an Extraverted mode, especially with raw emotions in play, this will indicate that a stress response is not far off.

The first stage of a major stress response will be an exaggeration of the Dominant function. So for a Dominant Introverted thinker, there will be snap judgements expressed in caustic tones with little or no data on which those judgements will have been based. As ISTPs journey further into their 'grip' response, they will tend to become increasingly cutting and vicious. With little or no data being gathered, there will be increasing failure of conscious, rational Thinking until the ISTP 'flips' into his or her Inferior Extraverted Feeling function.

Once this flip has occurred the Introverted thinker may become obsessive about using logic, may become overly sensitive to relationship issues and may become highly emotional. So ISTPs in the grip of their Inferior Extraverted Feeling will tend to become easily upset, whether or not they give expression to those emotions. They may feel profoundly alienated and may become seriously concerned that they have permanently lost control of their feelings and their emotions. They may express a passive-aggressive feeling of dissatisfaction, whining on in a petulant tone, and may be highly sensitive to any sign that they are being ignored or disregarded or even disliked.

It is most unusual for ISTPs to be able to reverse the flip directly and return to their Dominant function. For Dominant Introverted thinkers in the grip of Inferior Extraverted Feeling, one way out will be the use of the Tertiary iNtuition function – by 'getting up in the helicopter' and looking at the big picture, it should be possible to begin to see things more in perspective and gradually re-establish their equilibrium. ISTPs will need both physical and psychological space to make this adjustment, ideally being excused from some of their usual responsibilities – a conviction that they are unable to perform well will be common. In the often lonely exercise of Christian ministry the ISTP may need to seek such permission from a more senior colleague. It will be important that others do not ask how the ISTP is feeling.

Life-giving strategies

ISTPs are continually connecting to their five senses, are in tune with what is going on around them and tend to live in the absolute present. They are very great risk-takers, and because they live in the present they often do not see or heed warning signs. To become more effective, ISTPs will benefit from getting in touch with their own vulnerable side and accepting of it in others. A preparedness to put some effort into the people side of relationships as well as the task side, especially being prepared to ask for help from those they trust, will be beneficial.

Being opened to the less concrete will improve effectiveness – openness to the idea that a theory may have value, even if it is not possible to see any practical outcome. Being aware of harmony with work colleagues and being prepared to invest some effort in building relationships will also help. Exercising self-discipline in completing one task fully before moving on to another and sticking with a plan through to completion will be beneficial.

Opening up future horizons will also help; learning and applying techniques for planning and using conceptual Thinking about the future will help in the anticipation of problems and the development of potential solutions before things happen.

Summary

The cool, calm, confident, detached, independent, sometimes even ruthless ISTP is ready for anything – as long as it is exciting and challenging. Responding outstandingly well to emergency situations is a major strength. Leading through clear-eyed observation and analysis, with a gift for troubleshooting, the ISTP is a natural risk-taker. While team members will be allowed plenty of autonomy, there will be an emotional distance and poor performers will be dealt with ruthlessly. ISTPs will benefit from getting in touch with their own emotions, and those of others; from asking for help from those they trust and learning to look ahead.

3

Introducing the ESTP leader – the Energetic Problem-Solver

Dominant Extraverted Sensing with Introverted Thinking

———•◆•———

The overriding goal of an ESTP is to experience as much of the outer world as it is possible to do – to have an endless variety of sensory experiences. ESTPs focus on what is concrete, real and actual, valuing practical applications and facts, observing and remembering information gathered with their five senses and storing the details in their memories. They live in the present, trusting what they know from experience will work and distrusting intuitive insights.

* * *

Introduction

The ESTP preference is to work with lively, results-orientated people who value first-hand experience. They enjoy living 'on the edge' and can thrive in a risk-taking, adventurous environment. ESTPs are aware of the logical consequences of their actions, prefer to act rather than speak and will appear both open and flexible, while their preference will be for impulsive action. They value action, rapid change and taking risks. They are spontaneous and flexible and are keen observers. They are good team players and can respond in any given situation, making it work by being able to listen to a variety of opinions and take decisions based on logic, reason and a pragmatic view of what will work.

ESTPs are not good at being bored, at being told how to do their job, at having little or no factual information or at having restrictions placed on their freedom. Fun, flexibility and freedom are the three highly desirable ingredients for an ESTP. However, ESTPs are definitely the people to have around in a crisis because they cope with emergency situations superbly. Beware an ESTP in a routine situation for too long – there may be a temptation to create a crisis just to relieve the boredom.

Type dynamics show the Dominant function of ESTPs to be Extraverted Sensing – relishing the infinite variety of the material world and their interaction with it. The Auxiliary function of Introverted Thinking helps the ESTP to solve practical problems using logic and reason, cutting corners where necessary. The Tertiary function of Extraverted Feeling makes ESTPs aware of how their decisions may affect others and their values, and the Inferior function of Introverted iNtuition allows them to build a picture of the future inside their own heads.

The four functions are used in four steps, one after the other – Dominant, Auxiliary, Tertiary and Inferior – but it is an unconscious, and very fast, process. The Tertiary and Inferior functions may be used minimally or not at all. If used, they may be less well executed, or even omitted altogether, if they have undergone little or no development. Given a situation, then, to which a response is needed, the ESTP will first gather lots of information from the external world – facts, details, sights, smells, sounds, tastes and anything tactile to hand (Sensing). The processing of that information will then be by applying logic and reason and accessing any previous experiences that bear on the current one (Thinking). Once several possible solutions have been determined, consideration will be given to how each would impact the ESTP's own value system and the values and feelings of others (Feeling). Finally, an attempt will be made to fit this new situation into a wider context (iNtuition).

As team members, ESTPs bring enthusiasm, logic and a non-judgemental attitude when considering the suggestions of others. They also remember facts and are able to assess situations realistically. They may rely too heavily on improvisation and can be overhasty in coming out with their own point of view before they have considered the feelings of others. A refreshingly casual attitude towards bureaucracy, combined with spontaneity, flexibility and playfulness, can make the ESTP a highly desirable colleague.

With their ability to assess situations dispassionately and realistically, and their willingness to compromise in order to achieve a practical, workable, expedient solution, ESTPs are very valuable in problem-solving.

As leaders ESTPs will take charge readily, especially in a crisis situation, persuading others with a style that is both direct and assertive, having gathered facts and opinions and weighed up different courses of action. There can be a feeling of the ESTP moving from one crisis to the next and not finishing things he or she has started.

Comfort zone

The Extraversion preference of the ESTP means that energy will be drawn from the relational and vocal aspects of worship – ESTPs are likely to be fizzing after a morning of leading worship and may well relish the fellowship and interaction with members of the congregation following the services. The Sensing preference will incline ESTPs towards rich sensory experiences in worship – stunning onscreen audiovisuals, lavish sets of worship songs, a striking layout of furniture, lots of candles, colourful vestments, rich decorations. Ideally the worship style should be spontaneous and open-ended, with every possibility of following the movement of the Spirit.

Introverted Thinkers have a burning need to understand, to get to the bottom of things, to eradicate error for ever. This is most marked when Introverted Thinking is the Dominant function but is still present when it is the Auxiliary function. So in preaching and teaching, ESTPs will tend towards being factual (Sensing) and intellectual (Thinking), with concrete examples set out logically and unemotionally and with a clear list of things to do at the end. This may take the form of ways to change how one lives one's life as the conclusion of a sermon, or the home study to be undertaken at the end of a teaching module.

For the Extraverted pray-er God is revealed in the outer world of people, things and activities. While ESTPs may find too much silence daunting, they may enjoy some time in silence but spending time on inner-world processes will tend to be tiring. The Dominant Extraverted Sensing preference will incline ESTPs towards a simple, undramatic, down-to-earth spirituality, God being encountered through the five senses – beauty in nature, the wonder of creation, fine art, working with clay or painting, the perfume of flowers or incense, listening to music, the sounds of nature, experiencing the taste of bread and wine.

The Auxiliary Introverted Thinking preference will incline ESTPs to 'the prayer of reason', needing logic and reason in their prayer lives – they may well warm to St Thomas Aquinas. Thinking pray-ers tend to like structure and dislike repetition in their constant search for truth and meaning; for them God is truth. God will tend to be found in the mind and in past experience, the ESTP's spirituality being encountered as challenging in its search for justice, righteousness and truth.

Doctrine will be important to ESTPs, so continual theological study will tend to figure in their lives. This need to feed their minds will incline ESTPs towards using Bible study as a form of prayer – engaging deeply with Scripture in the traditional quiet time or perhaps using the classical form of Lectio Divina. While they may have an innate suspicion of emotionalism or numinous religious experiences, ESTPs may well experience charismatic prayer times.

The essential practicality of the Extraverted Sensor Thinker may well incline ESTPs to go into action from their prayer time as an entirely natural progression. The Extraversion preference will incline ESTPs to move into action on projects or tasks that give practical help – prayer in action. The Thinking preference will incline ESTPs to a constant search for truth and meaning, with God being found in the mind and in experience. ESTPs may well be challenged to search for justice, righteousness and truth. They will need to feed their minds in prayer, so Bible study actually becomes prayer. The perceiving preference may cause ESTPs to try lots of different paths and types of prayer, with God being a God of possibilities, of pleasures and fun. Remaining open to most possibilities and being comfortable with risk, ambiguity and eclecticism will be a hallmark of the ESTP prayer life.

When it comes to pastoral care, ESTPs have a finely honed gift of 'reading' people (Extraverted Sensing), picking up telltale signs in verbal and body language from those they encounter and understanding what their needs are (Introverted Thinking). Given their Extraversion preference, face-to-face pastoral visiting will be preferred and the smallest details concerning people they care about will be remembered, probably by reference to the ever-present notepad. They will gain energy from visiting people and following up new members of the congregation, and will find it refreshing to be out and about in the parish.

With their Extraverted Sensing preference, ESTPs will enjoy being involved in fabric issues. They will tend to notice the details of crumbling pillars, water damage on internal walls or the lightning conductor that has come adrift. If there is a re-ordering project to be undertaken, the Extraverted Sensing preference will lead ESTPs to become involved in the fine detail. The Tertiary Feeling preference, probably used in its Extraverted form, is likely to incline ESTPs towards seeing church fabric and re-ordering projects in the light of their contribution to the overall harmony of the church community.

Outside comfort zone

ESTPs are creatures of the present and see little or no value in thinking about the future. They may be very dismissive of developing vision statements and mission statements, preferring just to 'get on with it'. ESTPs who have worked in a corporate environment may well have had to undergo the discipline of forward planning and may accept that it has value, but this will tend to be an intellectual acceptance rather than an internal understanding that it is so. Especially in Christian ministry, where the Great Commission in Matthew 28 to 'go out and make disciples' is the overarching mission, ESTPs may consider anything more detailed to be a waste of time.

The preferences for Sensing and Thinking will incline ESTPs to keep things orderly and tidy and they will probably start out with an elegantly designed and highly logical administration and filing system. However, their Perceiving preference probably means that any systematic usage of such systems may well be abandoned when something more fun turns up. Routine tasks such as periodic returns to 'head office' – national centre, district, diocese – will be perceived as irksome.

The Extraverted Sensing preference will enjoy the interaction with people and the excitement of a 'here and now' experience, and the Introverted Thinking preference will enjoy the opportunity to analyse the proceedings for any errors. However, the time constraints of the meeting format and the need to reach closure on the various agenda items may well cause some problems for the Perceiving attitude of the ESTP.

Stress response

The 'triple crown' of fun, freedom and flexibility encapsulates the sort of working environment most congenial to the ESTP. A wide variety of tasks, with plenty of leeway in the use of the time and the way tasks are tackled, will be energizing. Working with others in a team environment, with freedom to interact with co-workers, will be preferred. Clarity about organizational structures, limits of authority, goals and objectives, especially if tasks allow the use of the ESTP's finely tuned memory, will be ideal.

Work begins to get stressful when deadlines are imposed or where conformity to a rigid set of rules and procedures is required, especially if that allows little free time; and being tied to commitments made by others with no leeway or flexibility will raise the stress levels. Vagueness about structures, authority and working procedures will be perceived as stressful, as will significant time spent on blue-sky thinking or long-term planning. Individuals with an SP preference very much live in the present and see no point in spending a lot of time thinking about the future – what will be will be and bridges can be crossed as you come to them. This does have a major drawback in that those with an SP preference will rarely see the stress building up; when they hit the wall, it will be a surprise.

As stress levels increase, the Dominant function becomes exaggerated. For the ESTP, whose Dominant is Extraverted Sensing, this will take the form of constant data gathering – hopping from one sensory experience to the next without the balance of the Auxiliary Thinking function to process and evaluate the data gathered. This lack of balance leads the ESTP into a dark place where the usual sunny and easygoing disposition disappears and data gathered begins to take on negative implications. The ESTP may become withdrawn, lose the ability to see the positive side and may seem preoccupied, worried and even exhausted.

When the 'flip' into Inferior Introverted iNtuition occurs, the ESTP can become overwhelmed by the unfamiliar – Sensing data will cease to be trusted; unfamiliar intuitive processes take over. The future becomes full of frightening possibilities. Fear and fantasy reign, with disasters, terminal illnesses, relationship meltdown; or grim forebodings of dire things happening to the nearest and dearest will fill the horizon. Because the ESTP is so unused to dealing with iNtuitions, any sensory data gathered will tend to be interpreted negatively. This particularly applies to intimate relationships, where the ESTP can read between the lines, read things wrong and attribute all sorts of hostile motives to his or her partner.

Extended periods of extreme stress may lead the ESTP into mystical highways and byways, searching for meaning in the esoteric. In this stage, ESTPs can present as a caricature of the sort of 'airy fairy' Introverted intuitive they would normally dismiss as being 'so heavenly minded as to be of no earthly use'. Extended periods of moderate stress will lead ESTPs into a persistently worried state, picking up any and every hint that others may feel they are not doing a good job, that they are being disapproved of and indeed that they are being viewed negatively. These misinterpretations are so out of character that close relatives and work colleagues may just wonder whether paranoia has set in.

The first rung on the ladder to recovery may well be the conscious use of the Tertiary Feeling function. If ESTPs can connect with their internal value system to see that such negative thinking is at odds with their normal well-grounded realism, and can see that they are disrupting the harmony of the groups of which they form part, they may be able to climb up to a more realistic evaluation of the data they are interpreting so negatively and thereby regain their equilibrium.

Life-giving strategies

ESTPs are essentially people of action – they move fast, talk fast and have a real flair for the stylish and the dramatic. Their preference is to live wholly in the present; they are impatient with the theoretical and see little or no value in it in their desire to get things done and dusted. The key life-giving strategy for ESTPs, therefore, is to downplay the joy and delight of their Dominant Extraverted Sensing and begin to develop and refine their Auxiliary Introverted Thinking – this could be encapsulated as getting out of the senses into the head. Unfortunately, this means thinking ahead – preparing ahead of time, considering the impact of opinions or actions and 'making haste slowly'.

As ever, an individual may find it next to impossible to do, think or feel in an unfamiliar, less preferred way, so may need to find a companion or colleague who can fill in his or her gaps. So in terms of communicating with others, ESTPs will benefit from preparing in advance what they are going to say and considering what impact that might have on those to whom it is delivered. This would be the norm for sermon preparation but time given to preparing for meetings, especially large public meetings, will not be time wasted.

Working in a team, it will be valuable to accept that others may need time to reflect before any action is taken and, indeed, it is important to understand that caution may well be the right response to a crisis situation. ESTPs will instinctively act first and think later; initial reflection may well be the right thing to do.

This caution may well also be the right thing to do when contemplating a significant change. ESTPs need to look ahead, beyond the quick fix, and consider all aspects of the current situation and the desired future state. It will also be important to take other people's feelings into account when planning and implementing a change. This is vital in the context of church because church sits so deep within people that changing anything will be perceived as a major, if not cataclysmic, disruption and upheaval.

When it comes to solving problems – the forte of the ESTP – a time of reflection will also be desirable. Recognizing that the first solution that works may not always be the best solution will be hard initially but will pay dividends if persevered with. Again, considering the impact that such a solution may have on others before leaping into action will make the ESTP more rounded and life more congenial.

'Stickability' is another characteristic that will need development. The inclination for an ESTP is to drop something when it ceases to be new and stimulating; the practice of sticking with something, even when it has ceased to be exciting, needs to be cultivated. Perseverance with something boring will be noticed, respected and even admired by others.

Summary

The even-tempered, good-humoured, optimistic, realistic, high-energy ESTP is ready for anything and wide open and welcoming for anything new. Leading by getting their hands dirty, ESTPs are intensely practical, keen to find quick solutions that do the job, and they will tell subordinates if their performance is not good enough. While they can be seen as materialistic and literal, ESTPs like to know where they stand, need clear guidelines and goals but also need freedom of action. Perceiving rules, regulations and routine as irksome, they can be in danger of making a drama out of a crisis. Superb in an emergency situation, ESTPs need to curb their inclination to create a crisis just to relieve the boredom. ESTPs will benefit from learning how to look and plan ahead, how to deliver tasks they have committed to, and from becoming aware of their own emotional needs and those of others with whom they work.

4

Introducing the ESTJ leader – the Efficient Organizer

Dominant Extraverted Thinking with Introverted Sensing

————◆•◉•◆————

ESTJs are go-getters – action-packed doers who use their energy and drive to complete concrete, practical tasks as quickly and efficiently as possible, often basing their solutions on what has worked in the past. Driven by logic and reason, ESTJs can be less than sensitive in their dealings with people but they are natural leaders who are quick, assertive and decisive.

* * *

Introduction

ESTJs are the guardians of tradition, inhabiting a world of facts, details and systems that they can acquire, examine and use with their five senses. They are analytical, logical decision-makers whose yardstick for credibility is their own experience. ESTJs need to be in a context of established policies and rules, and they enjoy developing and working to plans and schedules, which they base on established facts and procedures.

Type dynamics tell us that ESTJs have a Dominant function of Extraverted Thinking that they use to organize things to get the job done, and in short order. Their Auxiliary function of Introverted Sensing gives ESTJs an internal database of the things that have been important to them, which they can retrieve in a flash. The Tertiary Extraverted iNtuition function enables ESTJs to look at the big picture and see patterns and possibilities in the information they have acquired. The Inferior function of Introverted Feeling evaluates the decisions they make against their own internal values.

The four functions are used in four steps, one after the other – Dominant, Auxiliary, Tertiary and Inferior – but it is an unconscious, and very fast, process. The Tertiary and Inferior functions may be used minimally or not at all. If used, they may be less well executed, or even omitted altogether, if they have undergone little or no development. So in problem-solving, ESTJs will focus on organizing the resources they have available in the most effective way to address the issue at hand – now (Extraverted Thinking). Among those resources will be facts and details about similar situations that have previously been stored in the ESTJ's internal storage facility, accessed almost instantaneously and with pinpoint accuracy (Introverted Sensing). The situation can then be reviewed in a wider context, with a consideration of long-term consequences (Tertiary iNtuition). Only then will the potential solutions be filtered through the ESTJ's internal value system.

Among the types most likely to be workaholics, ESTJs have a well-developed work ethic that compels them to perform their duty and be responsible. They place a very high value on belonging to a group that is significant to them and they are conscientious to a fault – ask an ESTJ to do a task and you know that it will be done, and quickly to boot. ESTJs value right order and social stability – they know this is what will make people function well. With their attention to detail, patience and impartiality, ESTJs are ideal dispassionate under-takers of tasks. Dependable and responsible, with ample common sense, ESTJs are good time-managers who work to preserve the values of society.

ESTJs can become impatient with complications, finding the airy-fairy complexities dreamt up by their more iNtuitive colleagues irritating and irrelevant. ESTJs can become anxious about anticipated problems, finding ample evidence for concern in their internal database of similar situations in the past. While they are the backbone of any group of which they form a part, ESTJs will find that the most stressful thing for them is to be rejected by, or excluded from, such a group.

In a team context, ESTJs bring a down-to-earth practicality to the enterprise. They focus on the immediate present, on what they can experience with their five senses, and share their thoughts and ideas in a forthright, plain-speaking manner. They can be very blunt and forceful and have little or no patience for conceptual wool-gathering. ESTJs are committed to getting things done and bring drive and energy to the process, prodding their fellow team members to give of their best in pursuit of the goals. Task-focused and activist, ESTJs can be dismissive of people and process in their drive to get things done.

ESTJs are suspicious of any change, especially major change, and will need to be thoroughly convinced that it will work, often only if it can be demonstrated that something similar has worked before. Once convinced of the merits of a change, or if ordered to get it done by a senior authority figure, ESTJs can bring the necessary order and structure to the change process and will be willing to take hard decisions and get their hands dirty doing tasks that need doing. ESTJs naturally offer logical rationality to the process of problem-solving, and can be relied on to find the flaws in proposed solutions, often from a similar situation stored in their internal database. Similarly, they have a keen eye for the proper use of resources and abhor wastefulness.

As leaders (ESTJs are the archetypal armed-services leader), ESTJs take charge quickly and easily, readily accepting responsibility and bringing their experience of what has worked in the past to bear on a current situation. They bring order and a clear hierarchical structure, clarity about roles and responsibilities and systems for planning and scheduling. They can be guilty of micro-managing, of bossiness and of being hidebound by hierarchy and bureaucracy. Especially in senior positions, they can also be autocratic control freaks with a tendency to bully both subordinates and peers.

Comfort zone

Dominant Extraverted Thinkers like to organize things to get the job done – now. ESTJs will tend to approach their ministry as a series of tasks that they will deal with efficiently, get done and dusted in the shortest possible time. Social-action projects will appeal to ESTJs because they offer practical help to address real problems – shelter, food and clothing for the homeless and hungry, debt counselling, recycling electrical goods and furniture from affluent to needy homes. Often ESTJs will be active in planning and implementing such projects and they will typically be based on similar projects that are working or have worked elsewhere.

The Extraversion preference of the ESTJ means that energy will be drawn from the relational and vocal aspects of worship – ESTJs are likely to be fizzing after a morning of leading worship, with their Thinking function relishing the opportunity for intellectual interaction with members of the congregation following the services. The Sensing preference will incline ESTJs towards rich sensory experiences in worship – lavish wall-hangings, sound-and-light shows, a striking layout of furniture where this is possible, audiovisual displays or lots of candles, colourful vestments and a richly decorated worship space. The structure and form of a set liturgy will appeal to the Judging function of ESTJs and the repetitive nature of the weekly round will have a pleasing predictability.

Sensor Thinkers will tend to preach from the head rather than the heart. There will typically be a logical progression from point to point, coming to a well-reasoned conclusion. Sermons or talks will be informative rather than exciting but always well crafted. The intellectual satisfaction of preparing and delivering any form of teaching will be pleasing. Preaching to a large congregation or teaching large groups will tend to be tiring rather than energizing, but they will both be done with clarity and precision if not with charisma.

For the Extraverted pray-er, God is revealed in the outer world of people, things and activities. While ESTJs may find too much silence daunting, they may enjoy some time in silence but spending time on inner-world processes will tend to be tiring. The Thinking pray-er will like structure and dislike repetition. Intelligibility will be important, as will the exercise of logic and reason. The search for truth and meaning will be a continual one, and God tends to be found in the mind and in experience. The doctrine of the church to which the thinker belongs will be important. Bible study will actually become prayer in the classical sense of reading and meditating on the word. Emotionalism in worship or prayer, or numinous religious experiences, will be thought suspect. The orderly prayer preferred by the Judging pray-er will fit well with the Sensing preference. Well-organized prayer and worship times, with a logical structure, will be preferred. Familiarity will be preferred over novelty, and the use of set liturgical forms of prayer will be comforting. Order, structure and discipline will be very important, not only as the form that carries them through times of barrenness but also as a stable base on which a more open style can be built.

The Sensing preference gathers information using the five senses. An interest in church fabric will lead the Sensor to be aware of the state of the church fabric. In the Anglican Church there is a five-yearly inspection, the quinquennial inspection, by the church architect that results in a report detailing the actions that need to be taken – repairs done, gutters cleared, lightning conductors inspected and kept operational – over the following five years. The Sensor will tend to keep a keen eye on such issues. If the church needs to be decorated or if there is a re-ordering project, the Sensor will tend to be involved in and nourished by the fine detail.

The STJ preference will relish the order and structure of a well-run meeting. Standard operating procedures, standing instructions and the intricacies of meeting etiquette will be well in the comfort zone. Excursions from the agenda and lots of unstructured any other business will be found trying. The STJ with an Introversion preference will find meetings tiring rather than energizing, especially if the meeting is a large one. One can be sure that the ESTJ will be very well prepared for any meeting he or she attends, and woe betide anybody who challenges a memory about something important to that individual. The near-photographic memory and almost perfect recall of the Introverted Sensor will usually mean an uncanny level of accuracy.

The STJ preference will also enjoy concentrating on tasks that need doing, and administration may be an enjoyable aspect of working life. Planning of parish work, a timetable to be followed and lists of things that need to be done each day will be characteristic.

Outside comfort zone

ESTJs think carefully, rationally and logically and are able to spot logical flaws and inconsistencies very quickly. The development of a vision will not come naturally to the ESTJ as this tends to be the province of the iNtuitive Thinker. If the ESTJ is in a leadership position, there will be a need to find trusted colleagues who think creatively and imaginatively. ESTJs will be very good at building on new ideas, provided they trust the person who has generated those ideas, using their knowledge and experience of what has worked before.

The Sensing Thinking preference will make the emotional demands of ad hoc pastoral visiting less than congenial. Visiting people, individually or in groups, will be a duty rather than a pleasure. Meeting new people may be energizing if they offer opportunities for intellectual engagement.

The conduct of preparatory meetings for baptisms, funerals and weddings will be efficient and will get the job done. There will tend to be a lack of natural warmth and a focus on the nuts and bolts of the services themselves rather than the emotional human issues that will be around. It is likely that the occasional offices will be done to the general satisfaction of the 'consumers' but the use of the less preferred Feeling function will be tiring.

Stress response

ESTJs thrive in work environments that require them to take charge and bring their independent judgement to bear. They are committed to right order and will want to develop, and then work within, well-defined organizational structures where the most important thing is to meet targets and achieve goals. Work itself is typically affirming for ESTJs but they do like to have clarity about structures, roles and responsibilities. They like to work on practical, realistic, concrete tasks with well-defined deliverables that are tangible. ESTJs like predictability within an environment that allows them to work at their own pace.

If ESTJs begin to lose control over their own time and the tasks they are engaged in, work can start to become stressful. Lack of order, blurred roles and responsibilities and disorganization will cause ESTJs to perform less well than they would normally expect to, and their consequent increasing incompetence will add to the stress. If this is combined with a fluid environment where the smooth task-flow is often interrupted, or where ESTJs are required to work in a way that seems illogical, the stress levels will continue to increase.

The Auxiliary function of ESTJs is Introverted Feeling. A major characteristic of the Introverted Feeler is the need for life to be in harmony with his or her own internal value system. This deep, intense code will often lead Introverted Feelers to espouse one or more causes and to offer, and demand, intense loyalty. If and when something is at odds with this value system, it absolutely has to be put right. ESTJs are not good at showing how they feel, and they will certainly not advertise any passion they may feel about a cause they value highly. It will be very stressful for ESTJs if one of these core values is somehow violated – for example, if an ESTJ is passionately anti-vivisection and someone is being actively critical of a relevant demonstration or flippant about animal research, this will be perceived as extremely stressful and may trigger a 'grip' response.

ESTJs are not good at being demonstrative or at dealing with others who are quick to show their emotions. If ESTJs find themselves in a work environment where emotions run high, they will feel really uncomfortable and tend to exaggerate their rationality and objectivity. ESTJs tend to be somewhat blunt and insensitive in pointing out flaws or in taking the hard decisions that may have a significant negative impact on others. If their stress levels are already high, ESTJs may be plagued with memories of past decisions, comments or actions that have hurt others and become harshly self-critical. This too can trigger a grip response.

It is not unusual for individuals to overemphasize their Dominant function just before falling off the cliff into the grip of their Inferior function. ESTJs may become more and more detached and unemotional, act as coldly rational and dictatorial and make blunt pronouncements about snap decisions that have little or no data to support them. Rigidity of attitude and a withdrawal from emotional engagement with anybody may occur.

Once the Inferior function of Introverted Feeling has been triggered, ESTJs tend to become highly tuned to their own internal emotional responses and to those of others. Inoffensive remarks can be perceived as deeply wounding; any indication that they are not being valued will be taken as evidence of exclusion or rejection; and there may be some form of persecution complex. As they are so unused to using their Feeling function and expressing their emotions, when their feelings run high, ESTJs tend to overdo it – outbursts of fury, overbearing behaviour, cutting remarks. However, because ESTJs have such a high need to be in control, they may work extremely hard to disguise the fact that their emotions are running high, often saving their outbursts for the safety of home. Often ESTJs will be frightened or perplexed by these emotions surging through them and may feel that there is something wrong with them. This can lead to anxiety and depression.

As ever with a grip experience – being in the grip of the Inferior function – it is highly unlikely that individuals can get themselves out of the grip by their own efforts. A trusted friend – preferably an iNtuitive Feeler – to whom an ESTJ can unburden him- or herself, who will gently listen and not judge or intrude, will be a good first step. The way back to business as usual is to climb back up the ladder of functions – from the Inferior, through the Tertiary and Auxiliary, back to the Dominant. In order to regain equilibrium, an ESTJ should start with the Tertiary iNtuition function – hence the value of the iNtuitive Feeler as the friend in need. If ESTJs can be helped to see their current state in a wider context, possibly to see that their current behaviour actually violates their internal value system, and that a brighter future can lie ahead, this can be the first step on the journey back. Some time alone, some gentle physical activity, some appreciation of the beauty of nature can all bring in the ESTJ's Auxiliary Sensing function. Once that has been re-engaged, the ESTJ may be able to find some hard evidence that all is not lost, the picture is not all black, and finally can return to equilibrium with his or her Dominant Thinking function restored.

Life-giving strategies

It is reasonably common for ESTJs to have a very short grip experience because they have an innate ability to treat such episodes as yet another task to be tackled, and so develop strategies for themselves that minimize the impact of the experience.

It would benefit ESTJs to allow their feelings some expression in a controlled way – perhaps exploring their feelings for, and even with, those who are nearest and dearest or going with the emotional surge of a great symphony or love story. This might also help ESTJs be more gentle with people – both in a work context and in social intercourse. Working on their active listening skills would also help ESTJs in this endeavour.

Relinquishing some measure of control, sometimes even allowing life to pass by unplanned and being happy to be surprised by the unexpected, would help ESTJs be less uptight. Extraverting their Sensing function by trying out some creative pursuits, either actively or passively (painting, working with clay, art appreciation), might act as a mild release if tension is building. Taking a longer view, looking at future possibilities and not always insisting on what the rules demand might also help ESTJs be more balanced and less likely to pop.

Summary

ESTJs are forceful, practical, realistic, down to earth, logical and well-organized. They are very aware of rank and experience, are most comfortable with the status quo and play by the rules. Active and energetic, ESTJs like to be in charge, dislike ambiguity and see little merit in change, often characterizing it as change for change's sake. They view themselves as uncomplicated and straightforward and are proud that they call a spade a spade. ESTJs would benefit from getting more in touch not only with their own feelings but also the feelings of others, and from developing an internal monitor that assesses the impact of a remark or opinion before it is voiced. They would also do well to relax and accept that they cannot control everything.

5

Introducing the ISFJ leader – the Practical Helper

Dominant Introverted Sensing with Extraverted Feeling

ISFJs need to be helping others. They are patient, self-effacing and get along with almost everyone. They can be put upon and exploited but this can cause simmering resentment that may well all come out in a rush when the dam is breached.

* * *

Introduction

What the world encounters in the ISFJ is a calm, quiet, efficient exterior. Life is organized with a place for everything and everything in its place. Priorities are set according to their own personal values, often based on the people who are important to them – parishioners, family, friends, work colleagues – with themselves inevitably last. Conscientious and serious, ISFJs typically undervalue themselves and can be put upon by others. In a leadership position, ISFJs will expect to conform to the needs, structure and hierarchy of the organization, and will expect such compliance from those they lead. ISFJs will seek harmony with those they lead and will naturally lead from within – as part of the team – and will see themselves as first and foremost a member of the team.

ISFJs will avoid conflict where possible, or try to ignore it if not. Lack of clarity as to what is required, ambiguity, changes of direction and lack of control will all cause stress to the ISFJ. ISFJs need space and privacy for their work, with time for planning and positive affirmation that they are doing a good job. ISFJs will find it very hard to send anyone away if they are busy, especially if the caller presents as needing help.

In type dynamics, ISFJs' Dominant Introverted Sensing function leads them to trust and rely on their internal filing system of people who are significant in their lives. Their Auxiliary Extraverted Feeling function will mean that they organize the external world to care for people and their needs, while their Tertiary Introverted Thinking function helps them to evaluate realities. Their Inferior Extraverted iNtuitive function will help them to be more future-focused, making connections inside their heads and spotting possibilities in the long term.

The four functions are used in four steps, one after the other – Dominant, Auxiliary, Tertiary and Inferior – but it is an unconscious, and very fast, process. The Tertiary and Inferior functions may be used minimally or not at all. If used, they may be less well executed, or even omitted altogether, if they have undergone little or no development. So in problem-solving, ISFJs' first response will be to gather the facts with the five senses (Sensing) and process those facts in the light of their own value system, the values of those who may be involved in some way and the harmony of the group concerned (Feeling). They will then bring their logical faculties to bear to develop a rational solution (Thinking) before considering the situation in a wider context and looking at the big picture (iNtuition).

When working in a team, ISFJs are careful to listen and show consideration for the needs of others. They will tend to summarize and feed back accurate information and will always check the accuracy of any information they are given by other team members. They can become too focused on minutiae – facts and details. They make a great contribution to the team by being aware of past experience, what has worked and what has not worked, to provide a firm platform for the future. If change is in the air the ISFJ will support it if it is of practical value to others. Their thoroughness, organizational skills and task orientation will always be focused on benefiting others.

As a leader, the ISFJ will unassumingly help others in their work without a thought of confrontation, and will nurture and encourage others in the tasks they have before them. Once they have made a commitment, ISFJs will always honour what they have said they will do and will lead by example, showing others what it means to be thorough and painstaking, with every 'i' dotted and every 't' crossed.

Comfort zone

The ISFJ can be relied on to do what needs doing, quietly and practically, and to make sense of a lot of facts and details. He or she will tend to rely on tried and tested ways of doing things and solving problems, probably using a well-developed process that relies on careful advance preparation. The stable and efficient ISFJ will exercise his or her ministry with consistency and predictability.

ISFJs' preferences will incline them towards creating worship experiences that allow time and space for internal reflection and quiet contemplation (Introversion), concrete and practical hermeneutics in the sermon (Sensing), periods of silence to allow the message and the worship experience to be embedded with their value system (Feeling), and all done within the context of a structured and controlled liturgy (Judging).

For formal worship services, it is unlikely that the Sensing Judging mixture will lead the ISFJ to creative liturgical experimentation, and any changes to set liturgy would need to be thoroughly justified. It is likely that denominational requirements regarding worship will be known and adhered to. More informal worship, however, will be developed sensitively to allow different forms of worship to be experienced, but the forms will almost certainly be culled from other set liturgies, such as Iona, the Northumbria Community, Taizé. Home Communions will always be done 'by the book'.

Leading public worship will typically be quite tiring for the Introverted ISFJ but there will be comfort in the tried and tested forms of a formal liturgy. The ISFJ may become very distracted or annoyed by 'sloppy' worship, for example an assistant minister taking part in a service. The ISFJ may well be uncomfortable with 'open' free-flowing worship or prayer that feels out of control.

The ISFJ preference for Introversion makes it likely that there will be a preference for praying alone or in small groups. For the ISFJ, God is likely to be the 'still small voice' within; prayer is internal. God can be transcendent, unknowable, inaccessible and may be experienced first in silence and solitude. ISFJs may have difficulty with too much noise or action and their spirituality is experienced as 'personal'; so they may neither see the need nor have the desire to share their spirituality with others, and they may prefer to follow the text in their Bibles when lessons are being read in church. Retreat can be a source of refreshment – quiet meditation and contemplation in an atmosphere of silence and stillness.

ISFJs may want symbols explained before they can 'get going' on them, but may also fall into the trap of explaining them to iNtuitives, who might need to keep them unexplained. The ISFJ is inclined to work step by step towards spiritual growth and likes to be able to see details of progress.

With their Dominant Sensing function, ISFJs will tend to encounter God through the five senses – physical beauty, in people, in nature and in creation, and in art using clay or paint. The use of different bodily postures for different prayers may well enrich the ISFJ prayer experience; for example, standing with upraised open arms for worship and adoration, prostration for confession, open hands for thanksgiving, kneeling with hands open to receive for supplication. Flowers and incense in church or in private may be evocative, as may music, practical and applicable sermons and the physicality of the consecrated sacraments in the Eucharist. The Introverted Sensing function means that ISFJs may want or need to talk about details of what is happening in their spiritual lives, so will tend to have a spiritual director or prayer partner with whom to share.

Their Auxiliary Feeling function will incline ISFJs to find that Jesus is important to them, as will be other stories in the New Testament about love, compassion, sorrow, fear and trust. They will tend to experience God through relationships with people and things and to see God as redeemer, faithful one, life-giver, healer, reconciler and forgiver. The relationship to God will be very personal and very, if not supremely, important. Silence will be helpful in getting in touch with their feelings and there will be a need to develop their moral values as part of their spirituality. They are likely to grow best in an environment where people are actively and overtly valued, loved and wanted.

The SFJ preference will enjoy concentrating on tasks that need doing, especially those that involve serving people, and administration may be an enjoyable aspect of working life. Planning of parish work, a timetable to be followed and lists of things that need to be done each day will be characteristic.

Sensor Feelers will tend to preach from the head and the heart. There will typically be a logical progression from point to point, coming to a well-reasoned conclusion. Sermons or talks will be informative rather than exciting but always well crafted. The intellectual satisfaction of preparing and delivering any form of teaching will be pleasing. Preaching to a large congregation or teaching large groups will tend to be tiring rather than energizing, but they will both be done with clarity and precision if not with charisma.

The Sensing preference gathers information using the five senses. An interest in church fabric will lead the Sensor to be aware of the state of that fabric. In the Anglican Church there is a five-yearly inspection by the church architect that results in a report detailing the actions that need to be taken – repairs done, gutters cleared, lightning conductors inspected and kept operational – over the following five years. The Sensor will tend to keep a keen eye on such issues. If the church needs to be decorated or if there is a re-ordering project, the Sensor will tend to be involved in and nourished by the fine detail.

The SFJ preference will relish the order and structure of a well-run meeting that establishes and maintains harmony among those present. Standard operating procedures, standing instructions and the intricacies of meeting etiquette will be well in the comfort zone. Excursions from the agenda and lots of unstructured any other business will be found trying. The SFJ with an Introversion preference (the ISFJ) will find meetings tiring rather than energizing, especially if the meeting is a large one. One can be sure that the ISFJ will be very well prepared for any meeting he or she attends, and woe betide anybody who challenges a memory about something important to that individual. ISFJs' near-photographic memory and almost perfect recall will usually mean an uncanny level of accuracy.

The idea of doing something concrete to further the kingdom, especially something that has been proven to work somewhere else, will be attractive. Initiatives like city mission projects, night shelters for the homeless, breakfast clubs for street people or delivering gifts house by house to a street of homes will appeal greatly. Again, the Introversion preference will make such outwardly focused work tiring but it will be deeply satisfying.

While a preference for Introversion would usually make ad hoc pastoral visiting less than congenial, the Auxiliary Extraverted Feeling preference of the ISFJ brings in the care for people. Visiting people who need care and attention, individually or in groups, will still be tiring but the sense of a duty well done will be very comforting.

Outside comfort zone

ISFJs are not good at ducking and weaving, moving quickly or taking shortcuts, and may well obstruct progress by resisting change. They will tend to quote the rule book – Canon Law, denominational procedures, Prayer Book rubrics – relying on rules and regulations rather than being imaginative and taking risks. They tend not to offer helpful verbal feedback, tend to stick to the traditional, be very conscious of security issues and can be very stubborn.

Those with a preference for feeling are often said to be 'people people' – empathetic, encouraging and appreciative. They can take things to heart and be greatly hurt by criticism or lack of appreciation, which they may take very personally. Their great concern is for harmony, both external and internal, and the integrity of their own value systems.

The ISFJ thinks carefully, rationally and logically and is able to spot logical flaws and inconsistencies very quickly. The development of a vision will not come naturally to the ISFJ – this tends to be the province of the iNtuitive Thinker. If the ISFJ is in a leadership position there will be a need to find trusted colleagues who think creatively and imaginatively. ISFJs will be very good at building on new ideas, provided they trust the person who has generated those ideas, using their knowledge and experience of what has worked before.

The conduct of preparatory meetings for baptisms, funerals and weddings will be efficient and will get the job done. There will tend to be a lack of natural warmth and a focus on the nuts and bolts of the services themselves rather than the emotional human issues that will be around. It is likely that the occasional offices will be done to the general satisfaction of the 'consumers' but the use of the less preferred Extraversion and feeling functions will again be tiring.

Stress response

The Dominant Introverted Sensing of ISFJs will find environments stressful where standards, goals and priorities are vague or ill-defined, so that their very high personal standards of performance cannot be given their proper affirmation. Where they work with colleagues, ISFJs will also find it stressful where work done by others is not to their own high standards, thus impacting on the quality of their own work. Sudden changes, especially those not supported by reasoned argument, being asked to do things inefficiently or ineffectively and being asked to work off the cuff or imaginatively will also cause the ISFJ much stress.

The Dominant function of the ISFJ is Introverted Sensing. Using their preferred perceiving function of Sensing in their inner world, ISFJs absorb sensory information and experiences, reflect on them and remember, in great detail, the things that are important to them. ISFJs trust their senses; they trust experience, both past and present, and feel uncomfortable moving beyond sensory experience until it is thoroughly understood.

ISFJs apply themselves to facts and details, carefully and in an orderly fashion, and distrust people who treat facts in a cavalier way and are sloppy about details. ISFJs are responsible, conscientious and dependable and value traditions, organizational hierarchies and institutions. They give every appearance of being well grounded in reality, being totally trustworthy, and they enjoy finding ways of being efficient and cost-effective by perfecting the tried and trusted techniques.

The ideal working environment for ISFJs is one in which the focus is on facts and details, where they can organize those facts and details in pursuit of the goal. They like to complete one thing before moving on to another, preferably working in their own dedicated space with few interruptions. They will be happiest with organizational structures with clear reporting lines and operating procedures, and where expectations are explicit. They will function best where they are in control of their own work schedule, where they have little or no time pressure and are in a supportive structure that allows them to perform to their own high standards.

Life becomes stressful when deadlines are imposed and pursued, where incomplete, inadequate or downright shoddy work done by others affects the quality of their own work. A sudden change, especially one that appears to have no good reason, will be anathema. If asked to do something inefficiently, ineffectively, imaginatively or by the seat of their pants, this will cause stress.

As stress levels increase, Introverted Sensing types use the Dominant function more and more. Their Auxiliary Thinking preference – the judging process – will typically be less and less used. Like a dog with a bone, the Introverted Sensor will focus on more and more details and more and more facts and become unable to discriminate between relevant and irrelevant information. This leads to a significant loss of effectiveness and the 'flip' between Dominant and Inferior functions occurs. The Inferior Extraverted iNtuition has little or no control over facts or details, produces impulsive behaviour and leads to catastrophizing – imagining all sorts of dire future possibilities.

ISFJs' stress response will typically be to lose control over the facts and details of their lives, to become impulsive in their actions and to begin imagining all sorts of dire future possibilities. Everything will develop catastrophically, people will turn against them and life will be a disaster. This negativity and pessimism will be all-pervasive, and the usual willing response to requests for help will alternate with withdrawal and resistance to giving any help whatsoever. Others will be held to blame, the usual ISFJ accurate efficiency will deteriorate and nights will be spent tossing and turning, obsessively picking over problems. Ultimately the ISFJ will shut down and do nothing for extended periods before succumbing to depression.

When Introverted Sensors are in the grip of their Inferior function, negativity and pessimism predominate and there will be a see-saw between being open to the requests of others and withdrawal and resistance. Others will be blamed or accused of negativity, thoughtlessness or lack of caring, the usual efficiency and productivity of the Inferior Sensor will be absent and sleep will be hard to come by. There will usually be obsessive worrying at problems, sometimes fuelled by alcohol, until a state of stasis occurs. At this point the Introverted Sensor virtually shuts down, no work is done for extended periods and then depression sets in.

It is highly unusual for a 'reverse flip' to occur, flipping back to the Introverted Sensing norm. The Tertiary function is very valuable in these circumstances. The Tertiary function of the ISFJ – Thinking – can help to apply reason and logic to the extreme negativity and doom-mongering. With the seeking of concrete and specific reassurance of their own worth, their competence and their track record can come a reduction in the negativity. Tackling small projects, with the down-to-earth support of others, completing them and meeting goals can reinforce that sense of self-worth.

Getting away from the work environment, spending time alone drinking in the sensory delights of creation, can then be experienced as very healing.

Life-giving strategies

Personal gestures, such as glances, touch, thank yous, phone calls and letters, are important to Feelers, both to give and receive as signs of care and Christian concern. Church for them is about family, and harmony/disharmony will affect how they feel about it – they may suppress their own needs in favour of what they think other people want. If and when this diffidence and modesty is perceived to have been abused, it can cause the ISFJ to become resentful. Intentionally blowing their own trumpet about things they've done well, and de-personalizing critical comments – both given and received – will be life-enhancing, as will finding ways to voice anger and resentment in a dispassionate way, which will allow face to be saved by both giver and recipient.

With their need to find practical ways to help people, ISFJs find it very hard to refuse requests for help and can get over-whelmed by all the things they need to be doing for others. Cultivating a mental filter to identify pressures that can justifi-ably be resisted will help the ISFJ to manage his or her resources better. And instead of immediately jumping in to help, ISFJs would do well to heed the saying 'Experience is what you get just after you need it.' If ISFJs could relax enough to allow themselves to let others discover this, that would be good.

There is a short poem attributed variously to Frederick Langbridge and Dale Carnegie among others: 'two men looked out through prison bars, one saw mud the other saw stars'. ISFJs tend to focus on the details; learning how to look up and see the big picture will be rewarding. A more carefree approach to life, allowing themselves to go with the flow and have some fun without feeling there is a duty being shirked, will feel good – eventually.

Summary

The reliable, charming, helpful, modest and serious ISFJ has the patience of a saint and is there as a resource for people who would exasperate other types beyond measure. Leading inconspicuously and cautiously, with an emphasis on excellence, the ISFJ focuses on detail and on teamwork. Clear targets will be set, and people in the team will only ever be asked to do what the ISFJ is also willing to do. The wish to save others trouble may result in work being done that should be done by subordinates, and when an unpopular decision has been made, ISFJs will try very hard to avoid acting on it. ISFJs will benefit from learning to say 'no', letting others learn from their own experience, not taking criticism personally, learning to look at the big picture and occasionally going with the flow and having fun without the usual associated guilt.

6

Introducing the ISFP leader – the Versatile Supporter

Dominant Introverted Feeling with Extraverted Sensing

———————

The overriding goals of ISFPs are to develop an internal value system that underpins all that they are, to establish an external life that is in line with the values enshrined and to help both individuals and the world at large fulfil their potential. ISFPs are sympathetic, compassionate and accepting; they make decisions in the light of their personal values and want to serve others, but only on their own terms.

* * *

Introduction

ISFPs are the dark horses of the type world – it is highly unlikely that one will know what an ISFP is feeling or thinking. They present as flexible, open, mild-mannered and modest but also as quite complicated. Very self-contained and self-effacing, ISFPs are attuned to the five senses, closely aware of how things look, sound, smell, taste and feel. Often artistic, or with a well-developed aesthetic taste, ISFPs rejoice in the variety of creation and like to create things that appeal to the five senses. They are keenly aware of their own internal set of values and strive to live their lives in accordance with them.

Quiet and reserved, ISFPs are hard to get to know well. They are quite reticent in voicing their own ideas and opinions but are likely to be very aware of the emotional needs of others, especially their need for individuality, and will try to address them gently and sensitively. Typically they will want to be involved in a work environment that allows them the freedom to be themselves, where they will be faithful and diligent in doing what they have committed to do, provided those commitments concern people or things that matter to them. ISFPs often find it hard to be concerned about issues not of central importance to them, but when they feel strongly about something they will be adamant.

Type dynamics show that ISFPs have a Dominant function of Introverted Feeling, always filtering what they have received as sensory input through the mesh of their internal value system. The Auxiliary function is Extraverted Sensing, gathering information from the external world through the five senses. The Tertiary function is Introverted iNtuition, so they look for patterns and how the new information they have acquired fits into their overall world. Their Inferior function is Extraverted Thinking that focuses on organizing things to get the job done – now.

The four functions are used in four steps, one after the other – Dominant, Auxiliary, Tertiary and Inferior – but it is an unconscious, and very fast, process. The Tertiary and Inferior functions may be used minimally or not at all. If used, they may be less well executed, or even omitted altogether, if they have undergone little or no development. So when approaching a situation, ISFPs first consult their internal value system to gauge whether the situation is in line with their values or not (Introverted Feeling). Then further sensory information will be gathered to test and check the facts and the details (Extraverted Sensing). And then an attempt will be made to fit these new pieces into an overall pattern, and the possibilities explored conceptually (iNtuition). Finally, logic and reason will be applied to test and evaluate those possibilities (Extraverted Thinking).

Introverted Feelers typically feel passionately (but you will rarely see it), take sides and espouse causes near to their hearts. Once someone has gained their trust, and it will typically be someone who has taken the time to understand their values and their goals, ISFPs give – and demand – intense loyalty. If something is wrong according to their internal values, ISFPs feel driven to put it right.

As creatures of the present moment (Extraverted Sensing), ISFPs are always aware of the people and things around them in their outer world. Formal education methods – reading, listening to lectures, dealing with concepts – rarely work well with ISFPs. They learn best by seeing somebody do something and then copying them, by doing in the here and now.

ISFPs are very good in a crisis, when they will keep a cool head and do the necessary even in the face of physical danger. With little or no imagination (unless the Tertiary iNtuition is well-developed), ISFPs simply do not see the potential danger and wade in, usually to save somebody.

As a member of the team, the gentle and sensitive ISFP instinctively knows the 'word in season' that will make his or her fellow team members feel affirmed and supported, as well as being able to offer down-to-earth, practical suggestions. ISFPs may well be hesitant in voicing opinions or offering ideas, and may find long-range implications difficult to grasp because they are so engaged with the minutiae of the present. The caring face of the ISFP will be absolutely genuine and the ISFP shoulder will always be the one you will see others crying on. In a situation where there is a major change in prospect, ISFPs will always be attuned to the emotional needs of those involved and will be able to tolerate quite a high degree of ambiguity during a change process.

As a leader, the ISFP is committed to equality and collaboration and will quietly offer emotional support, allowing others the freedom to work in the way they prefer. ISFPs are reluctant to offer negative feedback, or at least offer it soon enough. Because they will always focus on the good in others, ISFPs may not always get the best from their fellow workers. They will often be very modest about their own gifts and skills, even appearing to be weak and indecisive.

Comfort zone

With their orientation towards Introversion, ISFPs prefer to pray alone or in small groups, and God will be encountered as intensely personal; St Paul's description in his letter to the Romans of the Holy Spirit dwelling inside us and interceding for us will resonate strongly with ISFPs. The Introverted Feeling preference will lead ISFPs to a silent style of prayer focused on people and the encountering of God through personal relationships. Biblical teaching is likely to be seminal in the development of ISFPs' internal value systems and, once established, will be a lodestone that guides them in their lives. The Gospel according to St Luke will probably be an ISFP favourite because of its attention to people and description of the compassion of Jesus. The Perceiving attitude of ISFPs will tend to make them open to all sorts of styles of prayer, and they will be happy to go with the flow rather than be locked into a routine.

Pastoral care is likely to be right at the heart of ISFPs' ministry. Their Dominant Introverted Feeling function gives ISFPs a genuine desire to help other people they value. Their tolerant and accepting nature means that they deal with people in a non-judgemental way, and their Auxiliary Extraverted Sensing function means that help given will not only be emotionally supportive but also very practical. ISFPs need to be aware that they may find it difficult to deal with people whose value systems are significantly at odds with their own.

The opportunities for pastoral care provided by the occasional offices of baptisms, weddings and funerals will be joyfully grasped by the ISFP. Care will need to be taken that the ISFP's emotional involvement in the life of a new baby, or the grieving process of a bereaved family, is kept within reasonable bounds. ISFPs will thoroughly enjoy the process of preparing a couple for their marriage, and the resulting service is likely to be very personal and even intimate. Baptism and funeral services are also likely to be individually tailored, with a strong personal thread running through them.

The passionate intensity generated by the ISFP's Dominant Introverted Feeling function, combined with an eye for practical details coming from the Auxiliary Extraverted Sensing function, may well lead ISFPs into very practical social action, providing help to people in the here and now, and could even develop into a significant force for social change.

Preaching and teaching by ISFPs will tend to be informed by their passion and intensity and their personal values (Introverted Feeling) but will also contain practical suggestions in following the way of Christ (Extraverted Sensing). With their orientation towards Introversion, ISFPs may find preaching and teaching draining, especially in the light of ISFPs' tendency to feel that their own gifts and skills are inadequate.

Church fabric may be of interest to ISFPs because their Auxiliary Extraverted Sensing preference helps them to be both observant of details and appreciative of the aesthetic qualities of a church building. However, an interest in a church's fabric is only likely to be kindled in an ISFP if the building itself has some emotional significance.

Outside comfort zone

Worship for ISFPs will ideally be internally focused and quiet, with periods of silence (Introverted Feeling) in a loosely defined, spontaneous and open-ended style (Perceiving attitude) but with something concrete to take away and work on (Extraverted Sensing). With their tendency towards self-effacement, ISFPs tend not to push themselves forward into a leadership role but may be happy to contribute something creative to a worship service, for example singing with a choir or worship band. They may also be able to bring their creativity to bear in the development of a service.

With their Auxiliary Extraverted Sensing preference giving them a rootedness in the present moment, ISFPs find it hard to be involved in any form of future planning. So the development of a church's vision statement, mission statements and strategic plans will be very draining. If the practical implications for the people involved can be spelled out, ISFPs may well be able to draw sufficient energy from their Dominant Introverted Feeling function to make a contribution to such a process.

Unless church meetings are concerned with things dear to an ISFP's heart, there is likely to be little enthusiasm, especially for routine meetings. Similarly, although the Extraverted Sensing preference will make the ISFP good at the practical details of administration, there is only likely to be an appetite for it if it can be seen to be of direct practical help to other people.

Stress response

ISFPs are driven by their internal value system and derive energy from work environments that allow them to work towards goals that accord with that system. This value system is orientated towards people, so the goals will preferably be focused on the well-being of people, communities or the world at large. Merely working for financial gain will not motivate an ISFP, and indeed may be perceived as stressful. Uncompetitive work environments where people get on with one another, and where they have time to work at their own pace without a high degree of personal interaction, will get the best from an ISFP, especially if his or her work efforts are affirmed and valued. ISFPs place a high value on unambiguous organizational structures, loyalty and security.

ISFPs will feel most energized by work that is focused on something that allows them to live out their own value system and where there is ample opportunity to offer help and affirmation to other people. If the work environment begins to get complicated, if ISFPs are required to multitask, especially under time pressure, and there is an atmosphere of conflict and interpersonal animosity, this will raise the stress levels. If this is combined with ISFPs being required to work constantly with other people, reporting in to superiors who are directive and aggressive, the stress will get greater and greater. Stress levels will peak for ISFPs if work politics require that they conform to an inimical set of values.

It is quite common for the Dominant function, in this case Introverted Feeling, to become more and more pronounced as stress levels increase. Any criticism will tend to be taken personally and Sensing data will often be ignored unless it reinforces the feeling of hurt. As ISFPs get more and more touchy, their normal easygoing nature becomes less and less apparent until the 'flip' into Extraverted Thinking occurs. ISFPs will then become coldly critical, very pernickety, and erupt in harshly critical observations about the emotional demands people are making on them, or pointing out the shortcomings of others.

ISFPs will also be overly sensitive to the possibility of their own incompetence. The untutored Extraverted Thinking function will cause the ISFP to be coldly rational and even combative. There may also be a strong desire to rush into action to correct an imagined fault. This may take the form of the ISFP assuming an authoritarian role and issuing commands right, left and centre.

Once ISFPs are in the grip of their Inferior Extraverted Thinking function, it may be possible just to wait it out until the storm blows over. If not, a friend or colleague may be able to encourage ISFPs' Tertiary iNtuition function to extricate themselves from the minutiae of the present moment and take a big-picture view of the situation. Having once ceased to be driven by the critical logic and reason of the Extraverted Thinking function, the Auxiliary Introverted Sensing function can be encouraged to recall facts and details that again affirm the ISFP in his or her own worth.

Life-giving strategies

ISFPs tend to be highly selective about the information they gather from the outer world, filtering such information so that only what supports their own ideas and values is recognized. This can lead to a certain self-centredness, and some conscious development of their Extraverted Sensing function will be beneficial, for example aimed at acquiring information non-selectively.

Developing their ability to share more of what is going on inside themselves will help ISFPs become less insular, as will canvassing the opinions of others in the process of making a decision. With their tight focus on the present, learning to look ahead, do some big-picture Thinking and coming to trust the development of plans and schedules, ISFPs will become easier to live and work with. This will be easier if the ISFP can find a trusted colleague who has a natural affinity for future possibilities. Having said that, ISFPs will benefit from becoming consciously aware of their inclination towards being too trusting.

ISFPs will benefit from using their Thinking function to analyse the information they have gathered with their Sensing function, instead of evaluating it solely on its consistency with their own value system. Similarly, learning to complete a task or project before embarking on the next because it is more interesting will be beneficial.

Summary

The self-contained, sensitive, artistic ISFP tends to have a deep spirituality that finds great comfort in the lasting values of a strong faith. Passionate, intense and quick-witted, ISFPs are gifted listeners with a genuine desire to be a listening ear and a practical help, accepting and valuing people as individuals. Very much creatures of the present moment, ISFPs look for harmony and deep relationship. This may draw them into relationships where they are absolutely certain of unconditional love, so they may well rest joyfully in the unconditional love of God.

7

Introducing the ESFP leader – the Enthusiastic Improviser

Dominant Extraverted Sensing with Introverted Feeling

————•◦•————

ESFPs are warm, open, fun-focused people who value others. They can be seen as lacking focus and prone to frivolity but the overriding goal of an ESFP is to experience as much as possible; to have an unending variety of Sensing experience that combines fellowship and fun.

* * *

Introduction

ESFPs live in the present moment. Any new experience is welcomed as stimulating and exciting but the ESFP is always practical and realistic. ESFPs have a great interest in people, showing great personal warmth to any and everybody. They are extremely talented at having a good time themselves and they certainly know how to make things fun for other people. Independence, resourcefulness and spontaneity characterize ESFPs and they have little time for structure, routine and forward planning. They tend to learn by doing and dislike theory and lengthy written explanations.

ESFPs are 'people people', with highly developed interpersonal skills, and they usually have a special bond with children and animals. Their appreciation for the good things in life –

those enjoyed with the senses – is usually strongly developed; fine art, beautiful music and crafted furniture will all appeal to ESFPs even though they may not have the money to acquire any themselves.

The ESFP's type dynamics show that the Dominant function is Extraverted Sensing – delighting in interaction with others, stimulated by that and by the whole range of sensory experiences. The Auxiliary function of Introverted Feeling means that ESFPs are guided by their own internal value system and by the needs of others in determining their priorities. The Tertiary Extraverted Thinking function enables ESFPs to think through the consequences of a possible course of action using reason and logic, and the Inferior function of Introverted iNtuition allows ESFPs to gain insights about people by picturing them in their minds.

The four functions are used in four steps, one after the other – Dominant, Auxiliary, Tertiary and Inferior – but it is an unconscious, and very fast, process. The Tertiary and Inferior functions may be used minimally or not at all. If used, they may be less well executed, or even omitted altogether, if they have undergone little or no development. In setting out to solve a problem or handle a situation, therefore, ESFPs will first gather lots of information from the external world – facts, details, sights, smells, sounds, tastes and anything tactile to hand (Sensing). They will process that information by considering the impact the data they have gathered has on their own value system and the values and feelings of others (Feeling). Then the application of logic and reason, and accessing any previous experiences that bear on the current situation, will help determine their course of action (Thinking). Finally, ESFPs will try to fit this new situation into a wider context (iNtuition).

In a team context, ESFPs prefer to work with colleagues who are adaptable, energetic and easygoing, in an environment that is aesthetically pleasing and values custom and tradition. ESFPs are free spirits who are friendly, diplomatic and aware of the needs of others. They like surprises and are happy to break the rules and bring a breath of fresh air into their work environment. Natural entertainers, ESFPs are very good at defusing atmospheres and breaking up tense situations with their enthusiasm, encouragement and a high good humour. There may be a danger of being viewed as frivolous.

Work for the ESFP can only be really enjoyable if it is fun, and work colleagues will be encouraged to play to their own strengths and value the strengths of their colleagues in their collaborative venture. ESFPs need to understand that they cannot always just wing it; that improvisation is a strength but that it should not be the normal mode of working. They also need to be aware that their focus on fun may irritate co-workers if that interferes with the completion of the tasks at hand.

Energy, spontaneity and adaptability are hallmarks of the ESFP, and he or she will joyfully embrace anything new or different. ESFPs make a valuable contribution by resisting the attempt by others to foreshorten problem-solving by accepting one of the first solutions developed. They are also very good at understanding and responding to the needs of others.

As leaders ESFPs combine energy with informality. They will ensure that every team member knows what their role is and lead by example in being productive themselves. With their natural warmth and sympathy they will motivate their fellow team members and they are committed to equal opportunities, keeping closely in touch with those they lead. The Sensor Feeler type inclines towards offering practical service of help to people, and will encourage those they lead to take responsibility for themselves in offering a similar service. Very much creatures of the present, ESFPs seek rapid results through collaborative working. They may be overly optimistic about the capabilities of some of their team but will find it hard to confront those who are not performing well.

Comfort zone

The Extraversion preference of the ESFP means that energy will be drawn from the relational and vocal aspects of worship – ESFPs are likely to be fizzing after a morning of leading worship and may well relish the fellowship and interaction with members of the congregation following the services. The Sensing preference will incline ESFPs towards rich sensory experiences in worship – a striking layout of furniture where this is possible, lots of candles, colourful vestments and a richly decorated church. Ideally the worship style should be spontaneous and open-ended, with every possibility of following the movement of the Spirit. Action with fun will be important to the ESFP, with a strong need to 'do' (dance, music, banners), especially with children involved.

The Dominant function of Extraverted Sensing will lead ESFPs to a simple, direct and uncomplicated preaching style, saying what they mean and meaning what they say. God may well be 'the God of the pots and pans', with down-to-earth examples. Introverted Feelers need to feel an inner harmony with their own internal values, not necessarily harmony in the groups of which they form part. So in preaching and teaching, ESFPs will tend towards being factual (Sensing) and focused on things that are important to them (Feeling), with concrete examples set out engagingly and possibly emotionally, but usually with a clear list of things to do at the end. This may take the form of ways to change how one lives one's life as the conclusion of a sermon, or the home study to be undertaken at the end of a teaching module.

For the Extraverted Sensor, God is revealed in the outer world of people, things and activities. The Extraverted Sensing prayer preference will incline ESFPs towards a simple, undramatic, down-to-earth spirituality, God being encountered through the five senses – beauty in nature, the wonder of creation, fine art, working with clay or paint, the perfume of flowers or incense, listening to music, the sounds of nature, experiencing the taste of bread and wine.

With their Auxiliary Introverted Feeling preference, ESFPs may be attracted to life in community, but the community needs to be the right one for them, one focused on the needs of others. ESFPs may find silence refreshing and renewing and enjoy some time in silence but as Extraverts may well find spending time on inner-world processes tiring. Bible stories about people will be preferred as prayer material, especially Gospel stories about Jesus and his love, compassion, sorrow, fear and trust. ESFPs need to feel loved and wanted, both by God and by the community of which they form part.

ESFPs are deep and intense people and will want to put right anything they perceive to be wrong. They also have a desire to give practical help to others, especially those oppressed by the unjust structures in society. Practical help in striving to change those structures, or to alleviate the suffering they cause, will be deeply satisfying to the ESFP. Initiatives such as a breakfast club or night shelter for the homeless, Emmaus communities that 'offer homeless people a home, work and the chance to rebuild their lives in a supportive environment' (<www.emmaus.org.uk>) or church-based shops or exchange schemes for goods and clothing will appeal greatly to ESFPs.

With their Dominant preference for Extraverted Sensing and their Auxiliary preference for Introverted Feeling, ESFPs will be revived and restored by parish visiting and will gain energy from meeting new people in the parish. Guilt will probably loom quite large in the life of ESFPs if other work pressures prevent them from seeing all the people who need their ministry. The internal value system of the ESFP will be extremely important, as will be loyalty both given and received, so any set of circumstances or any individual who violates either of these codes will find forgiveness very hard to come by. Confronting pastoral crises or dealing with awkward parishioners will come hard to the ESFP.

Outside comfort zone

Extraverted Sensors are rooted in the present and in what is going on around them. If asked to spend time in imaginative pursuits or contemplating the future, they will perceive this as stressful and not very much fun. ESFPs rely heavily on the past, the traditional, how things used to be, and often emphasize what has been lost – 'If only we could go back to the good old days'. They will tend to rely on what has worked before and will need to know the facts and the details, which makes speculative possibilities for the future very difficult to deal with.

With their Sensing and Feeling preferences so heavily orientated towards people, ESFPs will find administration irksome and a waste of time. With their Perceiving attitude giving them a strong disinclination for systems, planning, scheduling, structure and order, ESFPs may find themselves awash with paper in their working environment. Whether or not any given ESFP will tackle this problem head-on will depend on how important it is within his or her internal value system that the working environment is neat and tidy, with systems in place to keep it so.

Whether or not ESFPs enjoy the meetings process will depend very much on the purpose of the meeting. Meetings that are focused on the needs of individuals and how they can be met will be welcomed and enjoyed, although the ESFP chairperson will find it hard to bring closure to agenda items and ignore irrelevant diversions if they touch on the needs of others. Regular business meetings that focus on future plans will be a nightmare.

Stress response

ESFPs will look for fun, freedom in their working environment. A wide variety of tasks, with plenty of leeway in the use of time and the way tasks are tackled, will be energizing. Working with others in a team environment, with freedom to interact with co-workers, will be preferred. Clarity about organizational structures, limits of authority, goals and objectives, especially if tasks allow the use of the ESFP's finely tuned memory, will be ideal.

Work begins to get stressful when deadlines are imposed or where conformity to a rigid set of rules and procedures is required, especially if that allows little free time. Being tied to commitments made by others with no leeway or flexibility will raise the stress levels. Vagueness about structures, authority and working procedures will be perceived as stressful, as will significant time spent on blue-sky thinking or long-term planning. Individuals with an SP preference very much live in the present and see no point in spending a lot of time Thinking about the future – what will be will be and bridges can be crossed as you come to them. This does have a major drawback in that those with an SP preference will rarely see the stress building up; when they hit the wall, it will be a surprise.

As stress levels increase, the Dominant function becomes exaggerated. For the ESFP, whose Dominant is Extraverted Sensing, this will take the form of continual data gathering – hopping from one sensory experience to the next without the balance of the Auxiliary Feeling function to ground the data gathered in the ESFP's internal value system. For example, if an ESFP were to be leading a major building project with the pressures of time and money mounting up, the tendency would be to focus on the minutiae of the plans – perhaps continually changing the location of the toilet-roll holders – without regular affirmation that the new facility would be meeting a real need. This lack of balance leads ESFPs into a dark place where their usual sunny and easygoing disposition disappears and data gathered begins to take on negative implications. The ESFP may become withdrawn, lose the ability to see the positive side and may seem preoccupied, worried and even exhausted.

When the 'flip' into Inferior Introverted iNtuition occurs, the ESFP can become overwhelmed by the unfamiliar – Sensing data will cease to be trusted and unfamiliar intuitive processes will take over. The future becomes full of frightening possibilities. Fear and fantasy reign – disasters, terminal illnesses, relationship meltdown or grim forebodings of dire things happening to nearest and dearest will fill the horizon. Because the ESFP is so unused to dealing with iNtuitions, any sensory data gathered will tend to be interpreted negatively. This particularly applies to intimate relationships, where the ESFP can read between the lines, read things wrong and attribute all sorts of hostile motives to the partner.

Extended periods of extreme stress may lead the ESFP into mystical highways and byways, searching for meaning in the esoteric. In this stage, ESFPs can present as caricatures of the sort of airy-fairy Introverted intuitive they would normally dismiss as being 'So heavenly minded as to be of no earthly use'. Extended periods of moderate stress will lead ESFPs into a persistently worried state, picking up any and every hint that others may feel they are not doing a good job, that they are being disapproved of and indeed that they are being viewed negatively. These misinterpretations are so out of character that close relatives and work colleagues may just wonder whether paranoia has set in.

The first rung on the ladder to recovery may well be the conscious use of the Tertiary Thinking function. If ESFPs can bring their rational faculties to bear and evaluate their doom-laden, negative forebodings more realistically, they will begin to see that these are illogical and unsupported by facts. Once that process has started, they may be able to connect with their own internal value system to see that such negative thinking is at odds with their normal well-grounded realism. They will also see that they are disrupting the harmony of the groups of which they form part, and this should help them regain their equilibrium.

Life-giving strategies

ESFPs are essentially people of action – they move fast, talk fast and have a real flair for the stylish and the dramatic. Their preference is to live wholly in the present; they are impatient with the theoretical and see little or no value in it in their desire to get things done and dusted. The key life-giving strategy for ESFPs, therefore, is to downplay the joy and delight of their Dominant Extraverted Sensing and begin to develop and refine their Tertiary Feeling function – this could be encapsulated as getting out of the senses into the head. Unfortunately this means thinking ahead – preparing ahead of time, considering the impact of opinions or actions and 'making haste slowly'.

As ever, an individual may find it next to impossible to do, think or feel in an unfamiliar, less preferred way so may need to find a companion or colleague who can fill in his or her gaps. So in terms of communicating with others, ESFPs will benefit from preparing in advance what they are going to say and considering what impact that might have on those to whom it is delivered. This would be the norm for sermon preparation but time given to preparing for meetings, especially large public meetings, will not be time wasted.

Working in a team, it will be valuable to accept that others may need time to reflect before any action is taken and, indeed, it is important to understand that caution may well be the right response to a crisis situation. ESFPs will instinctively act first and think later; initial reflection may well be the right thing.

This caution may also be the right thing to do when contemplating a significant change. ESFPs need to look ahead, beyond the quick fix, and consider all aspects of the current situation and the desired future state. It will also be important to take other people's feelings into account when planning and implementing a change. This is vital in the context of church, because church sits so deep within people that changing anything will be perceived as major, if not cataclysmic.

When it comes to solving problems – the forte of the ESFP – a time of reflection will also be desirable. Recognizing that the first solution that works may not always be the best one will be hard initially but will pay dividends if persevered with. Again, considering the impact such a solution may have on others before leaping into action will make the ESFP more rounded and life more congenial.

'Stickability' is another characteristic that will need development. The inclination for an ESFP is to drop something when it ceases to be new and stimulating; the practice of sticking with something, even when it has ceased to be exciting, needs to be cultivated. Perseverance with something boring will be noticed, respected and even admired by others.

Summary

The sunny, optimistic, energetic, entertaining, generous ESFP is one of life's natural entertainers. They are happy multitasking, as long as the tasks are hands-on, practical, varied and involve people. Contributing to enjoyment of their own lives and the lives of others around them, their skill at practical problem-solving helps make life easier for others. As very egalitarian leaders, ESFPs ensure that people who work with and for them feel valued and capable; but they will have difficulty confronting poor performance. ESFPs will benefit from counting to ten before cracking a joke, focusing on the task at hand as well as the relationships involved, and only promising what is practicable. Some thought for the future will pay dividends, planning ahead and setting priorities, as will developing the ability to place the facts and details at their command into the big picture. Learning that feedback received is not always a personal attack will be a valuable lesson, as will developing the ability to give negative feedback. Learning to be more open to non-concrete ideas and concepts may be a by-product of learning to enjoy quiet contemplative time.

8

Introducing the ESFJ leader –
the Supportive Contributor

Dominant Extraverted Feeling with
Introverted Sensing

———————•:•◦•———————

ESFJs care deeply about people and use their five senses to gather information that they use to offer practical help that usually results in others feeling good about themselves. ESFJs are very good at reading people, collecting myriad pieces of sensory data that they store in an almost faultless internal storage and retrieval system if the people involved are important to them.

* * *

Introduction

ESFJs are sociable, gregarious, warm-hearted, efficient, always in a hurry and always with something to say; they could be characterized as Rabbit from the Winnie-the-Pooh stories. ESFJs work best in a cooperative, nurturing environment, where they can best serve the needs of others. They like to organize things and then work cooperatively to get tasks completed in an accurate and timely manner. They are very conscientious and very loyal, expect and want others to be the same, and value a stable and secure base.

Type dynamics tell us that ESFJs have a Dominant function of Extraverted Feeling that drives them to try and meet the practical needs of others and act decisively to make that happen. Their Auxiliary function is Introverted Sensing, using which ESFJs gather and store detailed information about people and things that are important to them. The Tertiary function of Extraverted iNtuition can help ESFJs develop intuitive insights about the capabilities of others. The Inferior function of Introverted Thinking helps them understand other people using logic and reason.

The four functions are used in four steps, one after the other – Dominant, Auxiliary, Tertiary and Inferior – but it is an unconscious, and very fast, process. The Tertiary and Inferior functions may be used minimally or not at all. If used, they may be less well executed, or even omitted altogether, if they have undergone little or no development. So in problem-solving, ESFJs will first and foremost place everything in the context of group harmony and explore how the presenting situation affects people (Extraverted Feeling). More information will be gathered using the five senses – posture, gestures, facial expressions, body language, tone of voice – to determine the emotional needs of those the ESFJs are with (Introverted Sensing). Further data will be gathered using the sixth sense to set the whole in the context of the big picture (iNtuition), before logic and reason are applied to test the possible solutions that have been developed (Introverted Thinking).

ESFJs are very traditional and find any form of change quite difficult. They are the ones who bring stability to their world and have a very well developed work ethic; ESFJs may well have a tendency to be workaholics. They feel driven to be responsible and perform their duty, whatever that might be. ESFJs have a strong need to belong to any group they view as significant and will work hard to earn that sense of belonging. One can always be sure that if one asks an ESFJ to undertake a task, it will be done. ESFJs prefer, and indeed need, a stable social structure that nurtures them and the groups of which they form part, and are convinced that they and others need right order so that they can function well.

Among their skills and qualities, ESFJs bring a patient, impartial attention to detail to whatever they undertake; they are dependable and responsible, with a great deal of common sense. They will be good at managing their own time, at making decisions and at obeying the rules. ESFJs will work hard to preserve the values of society. They tend to be impatient when things are made complicated and can worry about problems that are anticipated rather than actual. There may be a tendency for ESFJs to want to punish bad people and they will perceive most stress when they are rejected by or excluded from a group that is meaningful to them.

In a team environment, ESFJs will ensure that everybody's opinion has been heard (which will always be attributed), and they have great facility in organizing those opinions into a sequential and detailed whole. This allows the members of the team to stay on track. ESFJs are the backbone of any group of which they are a part and bring warmth, loyalty and stability to the enterprise. They will work hard at developing an atmosphere in which all the members of the team are quite clear about the role they play and how important they are to the team. If a major change is envisaged, ESFJs will instinctively resist but may well be able to bring a perspective based on what has worked before and will be very good at managing the everyday needs of others in the uncertainty and ambiguity of the change process.

With their Auxiliary Introverted Sensing preference giving them an almost faultless internal storage and retrieval system, ESFJs are able to retrieve and offer detailed examples of what has worked before to help their fellow team members develop new solutions. They will also be the ones who bring order, clarity and structure to the working environment.

ESFJs lead by example, seeking cooperation and consensus. They offer and demand loyalty – to the team and to one another – and expect each individual's best efforts. They will be keen to offer praise and affirmation for good performance but may go over the top in giving advice, being helpful and coming to the rescue. ESFJs are not too good at offering negative criticism, however constructive it might be, and may well handle conflict by putting their hands over their ears and going 'la-la-la' until the problem goes away.

Comfort zone

Their Dominant Extraverted Feeling function gives ESFJs a natural care and compassion that helps to make them among the most gifted of the types in the area of pastoral care. They have an instinctive gift of timing that helps them when the moment is right for a telephone call or a visit. The Extraversion preference means that ESFJs get their energy from being with people, so pastoral visiting is likely to figure large in ESFJs' ministry. Meeting new people in the parish and ensuring that they see those whom they intuitively know have emotional needs will also be energizing.

The Auxiliary Introverted Sensing preference will encourage ESFJs to do something practical to show their care and concern, so the ESFJ ministry is likely to develop along social action lines – expressing their love in tangible form. ESFJs are likely to be stimulated and excited by projects or initiatives such as food banks or city missions that focus on the needs of street people – providing food, toiletries, shoes and clothing for those who live rough will also appeal to ESFJs.

ESFJs strive to bring harmony to any parish situation and will be adept at providing emotional support for those in their care. They will find it highly rewarding to be involved in the emotional problems of those among whom they minister, and the needs of the members of the congregation and parish will be paramount for them, in some cases even overriding issues of right and wrong.

This focus on the emotional needs of others will be particularly true of the occasional offices of baptism, marriage and funerals. The opportunities for nurturing spiritual growth in baptism families and wedding couples will be seized with joy, as will the opportunities for pastoral care in the preparation, conduct and follow-up of a funeral service. ESFJs will need to have a strategy for handing on these families to other people, particularly those needing bereavement support.

The Extraversion preference will incline ESFJs towards worship styles that are relational and vocal; their Sensing preference will want concrete facts and details, as well as practical suggestions as to how they should live out their faith; their Feeling preference will respond to periods of silence and their judging preference will incline them towards structured and controlled forms of worship, so formal liturgies will be appealing. Leading worship, especially for large congregations, will be energizing given ESFJs' Extraversion preference, with their Dominant Extraverted Feeling function inclining them to meld the congregation together into a harmonious worshipping community. Opportunities for social interaction and fellowship as part of the worship experience will also be highly congenial to ESFJs.

Preaching and teaching will probably be a strength in ESFJs because their Introverted Sensing preference will facilitate their developing a practical message, usually based on something that has worked well before. The message will be couched in terms that will be easily understood – ESFJs know their congregations well – and will be focused on fellowship and meeting the needs of others.

Prayer for Extravert ESFJs will preferably be in a group or will be some form of communal prayer. God is likely to be encountered in the outer world, in and through people, an immanent, accessible God personally inspiring and energizing his creatures. The Extraversion preference will often mean that ESFJ insights and thoughts will not be fully formed until they have been talked through with other people. The prayer of Introverted Sensors is stimulated by their five senses and by their past experience. They may find that tactile prayer forms – clay, paint, music, pictures, the rosary – offer fertile ground for prayer. Symbols may be important but only if their meaning is clear. The Extraverted Feeling preference needs harmonious interrelationship with others, and that is where God will be found. Silence will be important – it will allow ESFJs to dwell on the wonder of relationship with God and with others. The personal value system of individuals with a Feeling preference will be a significant part of their spirituality. ESFJs are most likely to grow spiritually in an environment in which people are actively and overtly valued.

The Sensing preference combined with the Judging preference will incline ESFJs to order and method in administration. Filing systems are likely to be well thought out and effectively used and time will be managed well. The tasks that need doing will probably be listed and tackled in priority order – the priority usually being set by the needs of people. Planning will be a natural activity but will be focused on immediate needs and the needs of the short term – tactical rather than strategic planning. Their Judging preference will incline them towards detailed planning and sticking to a schedule, but again the Extraverted Feeling preference will always make these subservient to the needs of the flock. Meetings will be grasped as opportunities for fellowship and service and will tend to be energizing for Extraverted ESFJs. Everyday business meetings focused on the details of the present will be welcomed whereas future-focused planning meetings will be less congenial.

If the church fabric matters to ESFJs, their Sensing preference will make it easy for them to notice the details of maintenance work to be done, inspections to be carried out and repairs that are needed. These will be stored away in the ESFJ's internal database and actioned accordingly. ESFJs will usually enjoy the fellowship and the practical satisfaction of a physical job well done, of working parties to decorate the church buildings, tidy up the churchyard or clear out the church-hall store.

Outside comfort zone

With their Dominant Extraverted Feeling function driving their need for harmony, ESFJs dislike conflict and will go some way to avoid it. Difficult pastoral situations that require tough decisions, mediation that requires dispassionate rationality or thinking through the ramifications of the alternatives available (requiring the use of their Inferior Introverted Thinking) will be stressful for ESFJs.

ESFJs are susceptible to the temptation to become bossy and controlling, so unplanned situations, uncontrolled spontaneity in worship or disturbances in routine will be stressful for the ESFJ's Judging preference. Some rigidity of attitude may be exhibited by ESFJs if a suggestion or proposal is made that does not fit with the ESFJ's view of the world and how it should be – particularly if the benefits of the proposal do not accrue to the people the ESFJ considers deserving.

With their Sensing preference rooting them in the past and the present, and the combination of Sensing and Judging preferences firmly inclining them towards the status quo, ESFJs will find focusing on the future difficult and stressful. Visioning, mission statements, strategic planning and medium- to long-term goal setting will all make ESFJs uncomfortable and will be quite draining.

Stress response

ESFJs work best in an environment that allows them to live out their core values – one focused on altruism rather than profit and on making the world a better place. The contribution ESFJs want to make to society at large and to individuals and groups in particular will ideally be one that has little or no petty bureaucracy and allows, and celebrates, social interaction.

ESFJs are happy to accept responsibility and will be highly motivated to pursue the goals of the organization they work for, provided those goals are in line with their own values and principles. A variety of tasks within a clear reporting structure, with the opportunity for independent working, will be energizing. The key element of any working environment for ESFJs, however, is the people with whom they will want to feel connected and in tune. With their Dominant Extraverted Feeling function giving them a sharp focus on group harmony, ESFJs value others, and need to feel valued themselves, to give of their best. Recognition of their own individual contribution to the overall enterprise will be affirming and motivational for ESFJs; conversely, its absence will have a negative effect. Actively negative feedback may well be taken very personally by ESFJs.

Work will begin to become stressful if there is tension, conflict and interpersonal competition in the workplace. Equally, pressure on time that prevents ESFJs from doing as good a job as they would like to will be perceived as stressful. Lack of control, task overload and additional tasks assigned at the last minute will be very stressful. With their need to care for their own families, ESFJs may also perceive stress in their work–life balance.

If and when stress rises to unacceptable levels, ESFJs may exaggerate their Dominant Extraverted Feeling function and try to impose harmony and good feeling on their colleagues even if it is unwelcome. The inevitable negative response to this leads to ESFJs swapping their characteristic focus on people, their general optimism and their enthusiasm for the task at hand, for a withdrawn, listless pessimism and resigned martyrdom. If they 'flip' into the Inferior Introverted Thinking function, ESFJs can become highly critical, bossy and overbearing. Unconcerned about the emotional effect it will have, ESFJs can become aggressive, spiteful and coldly cutting. All too soon this negativity turns inwards, and ESFJs can become depressed and withdrawn and see no good in themselves whatever.

With their Tertiary iNtuition function unlikely to allow ESFJs to see themselves in a wider context, the Inferior Introverted Thinking function may develop logical analyses that are erroneous, make conspiracy theories seem persuasive and promote rigid and idiosyncratic thinking. There may also be an obsessional seeking after absolute truth, scouring the shelves of bookshops for self-help books that promise to give the reader the answer. While ESFJs would normally be the ones to be convening and running support groups, in the grip of their Inferior Introverted Thinking function they may well find solace in attending such groups and being assured that others are suffering a similar fate.

One way out of a 'grip' experience is to be encouraged to use the Tertiary function. ESFJs may find that in deliberately looking for a wider context – the big picture – and contemplating what futures might be possible, they are able to climb back up the ladder into their Auxiliary Introverted Sensing function to enjoy some solitary study time or the discipline of writing a journal, and this may help them get back in touch with their Feeling function. Similarly, talking through the issues with a third party, coming to understand that they cannot always improve people or enforce group harmony, and involving themselves in a new venture, may help ESFJs back to equilibrium.

Life-giving strategies

ESFJs will benefit from developing their less preferred functions of iNtuition and Thinking; learning a less intensely 'present' approach – taking the time to look for patterns or an underlying meaning in a set of factual details – and standing back emotionally to allow others to develop their own thinking. Group harmony is ideal for ESFJs, certainly, but it does not mean that no good can come from a slightly more abrasive atmosphere – it is the grit that stimulates the development of the pearl – and it is good to understand that people who work together do not always have to be friends. ESFJs would also do well to find it in them to handle conflict at an early stage. Equally, learning to take constructive criticism less personally, and trying to understand that personal improvement can come from accepting and responding to such criticism, can bring positive benefits.

ESFJs are good at empathizing with those among whom they minister and, therefore, can get very involved and caught up in others' emotional baggage. While this can be immensely affirming and may feed the ESFJ's need to help others, it can be emotionally draining if time out is not deliberately sought. Allowing themselves to plan-in periods of free time when there is no expectation of performance, and having a close friend to 'dump' on, can help ESFJs relax and just be.

ESFJs do have a tendency to know what is best for others and will want to rescue or reform them. They would benefit from listening more to what is being said and accepting that their rescue service may well be neither wanted nor appreciated. Also, ESFJs tend to find change threatening. If they can take a longer view of a prospective change and instead of simply dismissing the idea try to see the benefits that might accrue to others, ESFJs will find that the future may actually look quite exciting.

Summary

ESFJs are conscientious, dependable, warm-hearted, energetic and giving people who need affirmation from others to feel good about themselves. They are often forthright in expressing their firmly held views and have little tolerance for change. They are caregivers to a fault and will spend themselves in the practical service of others. ESFJs evolve their well-developed values from the outer world, and those who have been brought up in the context of a strongly ethical value system will tend to be very kind, selfless and generous. They will benefit from learning that the ratio of two ears to one mouth is a good guide to the amount of listening they should do as opposed to speaking, that people do not always need rescuing and that sometimes putting their own needs above those of others is the right thing to do.

9

Introducing the INFJ leader – the Insightful Visionary

Dominant Introverted iNtuition with Extraverted feeling

———————◆•◆•◆———————

INFJs are characterized by their patience, their creativity, their openness and their commitment to valuing people. They focus on possibilities, enjoy and trust their imagination, see patterns and meaning in facts and details and are orientated towards the future. The overriding goal of an INFJ is to understand human relationships in all their complexity.

* * *

Introduction

INFJs at their best present as imaginative and creative vision-aries, enjoying ideas and concepts in the abstract while being enthusiastic and committed to the needs of others. They are energized by their own inner world (Introversion), have a pref-erence for acquiring information by using their sixth sense rather than the other five (iNtuition) and for processing that information – and coming to decisions – using the feelings of others and the harmony of the groups of which they form part as a guide (Feeling). INFJs prefer to reach closure by coming to a decision rather than going with the flow, leaving things open and unresolved (Judging).

INFJs will see themselves as always searching for a perfection that has been lost and seek meaning and connection in their lives. They have a gift for developing an intuitive understanding of complex situations and human relationships. They trust their iNtuition and often find they are able to empathize with the feelings and motivations of others before they themselves know. It is often said that, having spent time with an individual with an NF preference, they will know far more about you than you do about them, but you know without a doubt that they are there for you. The most stressful thing for an INFJ is a loss of integrity.

The type dynamics of the INFJ show that the Dominant function is Introverted iNtuition, the Auxiliary function is Extraverted Feeling, the Tertiary function is Introverted Thinking and the Inferior function is Extraverted Sensing.

The four functions are used in four steps, one after the other – Dominant, Auxiliary, Tertiary and Inferior – but it is an unconscious, and very fast, process. The Tertiary and Inferior functions may be used minimally or not at all. If used, they may be less well executed, or even omitted altogether, if they have undergone little or no development. In problem-solving, then, INFJs will initially home in on their intuitive insights about people and their own images of future possibilities (iNtuition). They will then consider the harmony of the relevant group, the feelings of members of that group, their own feelings and possibly their own internal value system (Feeling). Then they will apply logic and reason to test their intuitive grasp of the situation (Thinking) before looking for some facts, figures and details to back up their analysis (Sensing).

Individuals with an NF preference have as their top priority their own self-actualization – 'I exist therefore I must become'. They value authenticity, integrity and their own identity, the uniqueness of individuals, alongside justice and harmony. And they are naturally empathetic, intuitive, great encouragers and are highly attuned to the possibilities of both people and institutions. Characteristically empathetic, these innovative individuals call forth the possibilities in other people and are also very good in a crisis.

With a tendency to become overinvolved and finding it very hard to say no, INFJs can be seen as unfocused. They also have difficulty with structure and with authority figures – they are the natural rebels in the type firmament. There is also a tendency to see their own values as the only ones, so they stick to them.

In a team environment, INFJs excel at absorbing and articulating the values of the team and at setting out a vision for the future. Their main contribution to the team is their conceptual creativity but this will usually be focused on people rather than tasks. They incline towards being conflict-averse and find being criticized as well as offering criticism difficult. INFJs' love of complexity and metaphor can make their communications to other team members more obscure than they need be.

With their people orientation, INFJs are very sensitive to the harmony of the group and will strive to build and nurture a work environment that encourages a team culture, mutual accountability and an awareness of where the team is heading. They may be guilty of setting too high a standard both for themselves and for other team members and may appear to be too focused on the self-actualization of other members of the team.

INFJs are able to use their iNtuition to provide useful insights on how any changes that might be contemplated are likely to affect those who might be involved but they also contribute high value with their stickability if objections are raised in the process of undertaking an innovative course of action. Innovation may be pursued by the INFJ just for the sake of it, even if an effective way of doing things is already in place. The ability to 'get up in the helicopter' and gain an overall perspective will be a major contribution of INFJs, in addition to their insights about the personal interactions within the group.

As leaders INFJs are future-focused and people-orientated. Their quiet, persistent approach, with their gentle reminders about the long-term objectives for those they lead, will tend to inspire their people to a collaborative and cooperative working style. Their own commitment to the vision, and their compassionate treatment of those they lead, will encourage rather than demand contributions from others. INFJs are reluctant to say the hard word and may ignore or overlook details in the present that are not in line with their vision for the future. While INFJs can be seen as democratic leaders, the experience of being led by an INFJ is that they know exactly where to go and how to get others to go with them; this can result in a feeling of coercion.

Comfort zone

With a rich inner life (Dominant Introverted iNtuition), the INFJ will be nourished by vision and new ideas – the big picture, what the future holds. The development of a parish vision statement, re-thinking the mission statement, strategic planning – these will all be meat and drink to the INFJ.

The Introverted INFJ will be energized and refreshed by spending time alone – either in prayer or reading and writing in the study. The INFJ's Introverted iNtuition will relish imaginative prayer styles such as the Ignatian practice of placing oneself inside a Gospel story and encountering Jesus. Unexplained symbology, intriguing sculptures, abstract pictures – these will all feed the iNtuitive preference. It has been asserted that 'The Inferior function is the undefended wicket-gate through which God can get.' As the INFJ's Inferior function is Extraverted Sensing, a prayer style that engages all the senses can be truly rich – for example, the classic Taizé candlelit service of Prayers

Around the Cross, with incense burning, biblical phrases sung over and over again in four-part harmony, a piece of recorded music, an artefact to handle, possibly even bread to share and a period of silence.

The iNtuitive INFJ will resonate strongly with the need to fit the gospel message to the culture of the day. In the Anglican Church the words used in the licensing of a new ministry encapsulate this: 'the Church is called upon to proclaim afresh [the gospel] in each generation' (from the Declaration of Assent). This idea of finding fresh insights into the good news or finding new ways of doing things in the church that will benefit those in their care will excite INFJs. Similar energy will encourage the INFJ in theological questions – finding answers to questions of faith that others find difficult and helping them gain new insights. The combination of iNtuitive Feeling will often allow the INFJ to get an overview of an issue or problem, and the INFJ will then be able to articulate that overarching view in a way that may be helpful to others. For some, however, the intensely conceptual nature of most of the INFJ's thinking will be very difficult.

With the iNtuitive's love of new ideas, change will usually be welcomed as exciting but there will be an awareness of the pain such change may cause others. Often seeing change as yet another opportunity for self-actualization or helping others in their development, INFJs will be happiest when they can influence the change envisaged. Designing a change-management process that focuses on group harmony and works at minimizing the pain for the targets of the change will appeal to the INFJ. However, as in all aspects of life, the INFJ needs to beware of the details or too much that is pure routine. There is always a danger of the INFJ overlooking important details or getting bored when things are too much the same.

Their Auxiliary Extraverted Feeling function will incline INFJs towards the people side of ministry. Pastoral care will come naturally and the needs of others will be central. Given their preference for Introversion, however, too many visits in a day or too many people encountered at once may begin to be stressful. It is easy to mistake an INFJ as an Extravert given that they Extravert their Feeling function. INFJs in ordained ministry are typically averse to conflict and will go to great lengths to avoid confrontation with parishioners or colleagues. The INFJ's Feeling preference will tend to make INFJ ministers highly sensitive to the emotional undercurrents in a pastoral situation, and they will tend to respond with great compassion and an attempt to meet the needs of their parishioners. They will find it rewarding to deal with the emotional problems they encounter and enjoy the feeling of being part of a harmonious whole.

The Feeling preference, combined with the visionary orientation of the iNtuitive, will make the INFJ happiest when creating a nurturing framework for the future of the parish, sector or area of responsibility. Because they will always be seeking to become better people and to encourage those around them, INFJs will be keen to develop others, especially if they are responsible for training more junior clergy. This may take the form of coaching, which INFJs may find difficult with their instinctive, intuitive knowledge of their coachee – the non-directive approach of the coach will be frustrating for an INFJ to maintain ('It's as plain as the nose on your face'). The INFJ's Feeling function will occasionally lead to overly sensitive handling of performance issues – indeed, the INFJ may be experienced as generous with his or her praise but wishy-washy in dealing with underachievement.

The INFJ's Judging orientation prefers order and structure, so leading worship in the context of a familiar liturgy will typically be done well. The combination of iNtuition with Feeling will lead to preaching that tends to be inspirational and visionary – people-centred sermons that paint a big picture of how things might be and how good that might feel. Often these will be concluded with a challenge to some form of self-improvement – or at least openness to God's transforming power – often in the form of a question. The preference for Introversion will often mean that this essentially Extraverted activity will be emotionally draining – a significant amount of emotional energy will have been expended in leading public worship and preaching, so there will usually be a need for the INFJ to have a time of rest and quiet after a morning's services. Teaching and training, either within the parish context or extra-curricularly, will also be strengths. Leading small groups will be emotionally satisfying for INFJs, but given their constant striving for self-actualization, always with the caveat that they should not get overinvolved in the emotional issues of the group's members.

While meetings will be draining in a similar way to leading worship, chairing meetings such as, within the Anglican tradition, the parochial church council or the annual parochial church meeting will be comfortable for the INFJ. The Judging orientation will be at home with the order and structure of the agenda; the Feeling function will be sensitive to the emotional undercurrents among those present and will strive for harmony. The iNtuiting function will be able to hear the music, not just the words in the interplay between those attending the meeting. This will allow opportunities for enabling and facilitating the contributions of the more reticent and the avoidance of too many excursions into territory more properly the concern of another forum – particularly where there is a tendency to repeat work already done at an inappropriate level of detail.

The INFJ's Judging preference will need plans and schedules for comfort. Worship services should start on time and follow the planned structure (although the iNtuitive preference may have planned-in something just a little different this week). The INFJ will often need the reassurance of a to-do list.

Outside comfort zone

The iNtuitive INFJ will find it difficult to engage with practical details. The church building's state of repair, the fine detail of a re-ordering or the minutiae of a Health and Safety inspection will leave the INFJ cold. In fact it would be hazardous to leave such important elements to the INFJ minister because the details will tend to be skipped over – or skimped on – as the INFJ's imagination soars on to the next big-picture possibility.

A similar lesson can be learned about the routine of administration. INFJs will tend to employ a 'piling system' – they will know exactly in which of the many piles of paper in their study is the item being sought, and woe betide the one who tidies up the piles. The INFJ's Judging preference will find going with the flow difficult.

INFJs find it all too easy to soar away on flights of fancy and ignore the practical implications of the creative ideas. They also find it very difficult to offer constructive criticism until it is almost too late. With a marked desire to be liked and to achieve a harmonious atmosphere at all costs, INFJs find it hard to confront disputes or take tough decisions. The consequences of any action will always be viewed in emotional terms, and INFJs can get overly involved emotionally, when their empathy with others can cause them a degree of grief. Any criticism they receive will be taken by INFJs as very personal and potentially very hurtful.

INFJs find it hard to share, explain and discuss their visionary ideas but would benefit greatly from doing so. They also find it difficult to have their routine upset and find unexpected intrusions hard to handle.

Stress response

With their Dominant function of Introverted iNtuition, INFJs find the best working environment to be one that is under their control and both values and encourages their future-orientated creativity. They want their gifts and skills to be recognized and used and are most comfortable in tackling a variety of tasks in an environment that has clear structures, where work can be scheduled flexibly and there is a good deal of autonomy. A clearly defined role and clearly defined boundaries and expectations will be energizing. An environment that is organized, well structured and with no surprises, with fellow team members they can nurture and encourage and where it is possible to achieve closure, will get the best from INFJs.

Things will start to go awry if the INFJ is required to deal with significant amounts of detail, especially if it is in the outer world. Too much time in the outer world – being required to be Extraverted for extended periods – will begin to be stressful. Being required to work as a subordinate to people who are unfeeling or dishonest – or alongside fellow workers who leave things half done or whose performance leaves a lot to be desired – will cause increasing amounts of stress.

A work environment that is disorganized, crowded and noisy will be difficult for the INFJ. It has to be said that 'disorganized' does not necessarily mean untidy. Another major stressor is being asked to compromise on personal high standards and principles or to be party to deceit or dishonesty.

One can tell when an INFJ is stressed – the 'flip' into the Inferior function occurs, and that Inferior function, Sensing, will take over. INFJs will tend to become completely absorbed in trivial detail – the fine detail of the layout of a document, getting to the next level in a computer game, the need to order books on a shelf by height – and ignore the major issue facing them. The usually fastidious INFJ may become sloppy and careless and, although never overly aware of the feelings of others, will tell it like it is in a curt and highly critical manner. It may become very important that a particular drawer in the filing cabinet be tidied up, or cleaning the PC screen may become paramount.

The classic INFJ stress response, however, is overindulgence in sensory pleasures. Bouts of hedonistic indulgence – overeating, smoking, drinking heavily, watching too much television, recreational drug abuse – will inevitably be followed by feelings of self-loathing, which may trigger further such bouts to dull the pain.

Life-giving strategies

For INFJs to be more at peace with themselves and more in tune with those among whom they minister, they need to withdraw and take time alone to recharge their batteries; gentle exercise will repay dividends. If the Feeling function can be moderated – early mention of inadequate performance to a fellow worker, trying to take criticism less personally, holding back on the apology – life can become easier.

In their dealings with others – fellow shepherds or flock – a less demanding approach will bear fruit. Finding a way to say the necessary negative sooner rather than later – constructive criticisms as opposed to constant praise and encouragement – will actually be acceptable to the recipients, if not something of a relief. If the INFJ can genuinely involve and consult others, sharing ideas and chewing them through, this can help make for better decisions.

The need for constant improvement also needs to be reined in. Cultivating a fit-for-purpose attitude – 'Is this good *enough?*' – will relieve the pressure to perform. If the bar is constantly being raised, with yet higher standards being demanded, this can create an exhausting environment. Sometimes it might pay to postpone a decision – to go with the flow. Given the blind spot INFJs have about details, and their impatience with them, ensuring that someone who *is* good at detail has done the necessary preparatory work before a decision is taken may lead to better decisions in the long run.

INFJs have a tendency to strive for self-actualization, always seeking to be a better person, so finding something to do for relaxation that does not entail constant self-improvement or demand high levels of application and concentration will be life-enhancing.

Summary

The patient, innovative, empathetic, stubborn and enigmatic INFJ strives to understand people and their interaction. INFJs are committed to integrity and to collaborative working. They listen carefully, nurture those among whom they work and find injustice and practical jokes distasteful. To develop to their full potential, INFJs will benefit from grounding their visions in practical reality and taking justified criticism less personally. If they can internalize the fact that it is the piece of grit in the oyster that makes the pearl, INFJs will benefit from understanding that conflict can be creative and that constructive feedback given early may be highly beneficial.

10

Introducing the INFP leader – the Thoughtful Idealist

Dominant Introverted Feeling with Extraverted iNtuition

———◆———

The overriding goal of the idealistic INFP is to make the world a better place for people. Caring and considerate, if somewhat reserved, INFPs are good listeners who have an intuitive understanding of – and try to meet – the needs of those they encounter.

* * *

Introduction

INFPs are driven by their internal value system and their own moral code. They present as idealistic, open-minded (as long as a new situation does not go against their values, when they can become stubborn and intransigent), flexible and enthusiastic. They are averse to conflict and will go a long way to avoid it. If facing conflict is inevitable, it will always be evaluated with the heart, focusing on how it makes them feel rather than the rights and wrongs of the situation. From one viewpoint, this can make INFPs appear inconsistent or irrational but, from another, it makes them very talented mediators with their instinctive understanding of the way each party to the dispute feels.

INFPs work best in an environment that is quiet, calm and free of bureaucratic overkill. Their work rate will increase substantially if the task on which they are engaged is in line with their own internal values. Typically they will want to be involved in a work environment that contributes not only to their own growth and development but also to that of others. They dislike impersonal treatment, negative feedback, competition and any feeling that they might have let somebody else down. A harmonious, cooperative working environment where the INFP can be autonomous and private, regularly receiving positive affirmation, will be energizing.

In a team environment, INFPs contribute to the harmony and cohesion of the team by being sensitive listeners and positive encouragers. They also have a talent for presenting what might be quite challenging ideas in a big-picture context because they have a keen sense of the emotional impact those ideas may have. INFPs are keen to see fellow team members grow and develop and will motivate and inspire others to self-improvement. Building team morale will be done by an INFP discerning and articulating common ideals and values. INFPs can be blissfully unaware of hierarchical structures and may also fight their corner to promote and defend an ideal that has little or no support among the rest of the team.

Where a major change is contemplated, INFPs are good at motivating others to take a number of different viewpoints about the proposed change and will typically be innovative, imaginative and creative. They may be guilty of spending too long exploring the possibilities of the proposed change, thereby slowing down progress, and may be too focused on the feelings of others rather than contributing to expedient closure. This tendency may well be a strength in solving problems or resolving conflicts because INFPs are able to build consensus among the team and broker compromise solutions that are acceptable to all.

As leaders INFPs can be inspirational, working as part of the team and establishing a non-directive structure that gives their subordinates freedom to develop within a supportive framework underpinned by the INFP's vision of what is possible and commitment to nurturing the team dynamics. INFPs would far rather praise than criticize and may be guilty of working around problems rather than confronting them.

Type dynamics show that INFPs have a Dominant function of Introverted Feeling, where inner harmony with their own value system is paramount. The Auxiliary function is Extraverted iNtuition, which gives them the ability to see possibilities in the present for future development. The Tertiary function is Introverted Sensing, connecting INFPs to their five senses and helping them to be in tune with what is going on around them. Finally the Inferior function is Extraverted Thinking that focuses on getting the job done for now and seeing people as there to do the job, giving a high task orientation.

The four functions are used in four steps, one after the other – Dominant, Auxiliary, Tertiary and Inferior – but it is an unconscious, and very fast, process. The Tertiary and Inferior functions may be used minimally or not at all. If used, they may be less well executed, or even omitted altogether, if they have undergone little or no development. So in decision-making, INFPs first consult their internal value system to assess the situation in the light of their own values (Introverted Feeling). Then they will look at future possibilities and patterns (Extraverted iNtuition). The Tertiary Sensing function can then be deployed to look at the facts and acquire the details of the situation before the Inferior function of Extraverted Thinking applies logic and reason to develop a practical solution.

Comfort zone

INFPs' Dominant Introverted Feeling function gives them a genuine desire to help other people, so pastoral care is likely to be the centre of an INFP's ministry. Their tolerant and accepting nature means that INFPs deal with people in a non-judgemental way and their Auxiliary Extraverted iNtuition function means that help given will not only be emotionally supportive but also focused on the needs they have intuitively recognized. INFPs need to be aware that they may find it difficult to deal with people whose value systems are significantly at odds with their own.

The opportunities for pastoral care provided by the occasional offices of baptisms, weddings and funerals will appeal greatly to the INFP. Care will need to be taken that the INFP's emotional involvement in the life of a new baby or the grieving process of a bereaved family is kept within reasonable bounds. INFPs will thoroughly enjoy the process of preparing a couple for their marriage and the resulting service is likely to be very personal and even intimate. Baptism and funeral services are also likely to be individually tailored, with a strong personal thread running through them.

The Auxiliary Extraverted iNtuition function will energize INFPs in their sermon preparation as they pursue their quest for fresh gospel truths, for developing new ways of addressing the hard questions of faith and in the preparation of intriguing questions with which to leave their congregations. INFPs will also have energy to spare for big-picture thinking about the direction of their church and its congregation. The world of vision statements, their church's mission and the strategic goals towards which it is working will be stimulating and energizing for INFPs, provided the focus is on addressing the needs of the people to whom they minister.

With their Perceiving preference, flexibility and variety will be important to INFPs – 'Don't fence me in.' Variations in worship services and openness to the movement of the Spirit will be energizing, as will the new and unexpected in everyday ministry; anything that promises to break the routine of a day will be welcomed. The likelihood that a people-focused ministry will make each day different will be music to the INFP's ears.

With their orientation towards Introversion, INFPs will find praying alone or in small groups refreshing, and God will be encountered as intensely personal; St Paul's description in his letter to the Romans of the Holy Spirit dwelling inside us and interceding for us will resonate strongly with INFPs. The Introverted Feeling preference will lead INFPs to a silent style of prayer focused on people and the encountering of God through personal relationships. Biblical teaching is likely to be seminal in the development of the INFP's internal value system and, once established, will be a lodestone that guides the INFP in life. The Gospel according to St Luke will probably be an INFP favourite because of its attention to people and description of the compassion of Jesus. The Perceiving attitude of INFPs will tend to make them open to all sorts of styles of prayer, and they will be happy to go with the flow rather than be locked into a routine.

Outside comfort zone

Worship for INFPs will ideally be internally focused and quiet, with periods of silence (Introverted Feeling), in a loosely defined, spontaneous and open-ended style (Perceiving attitude) but with a vision of exciting possibilities for the future (Extraverted iNtuition). With their tendency towards self-effacement, INFPs tend not to push themselves forward into a leadership role but may be happy to contribute something creative to a worship service, such as creating beautiful banners to decorate the church and emphasize the theme of the service. They may also be able to bring their creativity to bear in developing a service. If required to lead worship, this will tend to be very draining.

The INFP Introverted Feeling preference will tend to make dealing with large numbers of people, either together or one after the other, draining; there will be a tendency to prefer ministering on a one-to-one basis with time for reflection and recharging in between encounters. Similarly, the need to focus on tasks that need to be done, forms to be completed, returns to be made, especially when that entails dealing with significant amounts of detail, will also drain rather than energize INFPs (Auxiliary Extraverted iNtuition). Concern with church fabric, regular electrical equipment testing, checking of fire extinguishers or the daily round of church administration will not appeal to INFPs. Unless church meetings are concerned with things dear to an INFP's heart, there is likely to be little enthusiasm, especially for routine meetings. The same will be true of detailed planning or tight scheduling – INFPs will much prefer to go with the flow.

With their Dominant Introverted Feeling function, INFPs will try to avoid conflict; if their pastoral encounters raise difficult interpersonal issues, INFPs will seek to restore harmony rather than insist on sticking to principle. The exception is likely to be a situation where their own internal values are compromised, when they can become unexpectedly stubborn and inflexible.

While INFPs will be deeply concerned with meeting the needs of others, and may have dozens of ideas about how these might be met (grand visions of collaborative care, projects to shelter and nurture drug addicts or street people, mutual self-help schemes), social action will always preferably be done by other people – INFPs much prefer the 'doing' to be done by others.

Stress response

INFPs are driven by their internal value system and derive energy from work environments that allow them to move towards goals that accord with that system. This value system is orientated towards people, so the goals will preferably be focused on the well-being of people, communities or the world at large. Merely working for financial gain will not motivate an INFP, and indeed may be perceived as stressful, although INFPs are comfortable with achieving work goals and expressing themselves through their work. Uncompetitive work environments where people get on with one another, and where they have time to work at their own pace without a high degree of personal interaction, will get the best from INFPs, especially if their work efforts are affirmed and valued. They place a high value on unambiguous organizational structures, loyalty and security.

INFPs will feel most energized by work that is focused on something that allows them to live out their own value system and where there is ample opportunity to offer help and affirmation to other people. If the work environment begins to get complicated – if INFPs are required to multitask, especially under time pressure, and there is an atmosphere of conflict and interpersonal animosity – this will raise the stress levels. If this is combined with INFPs being required to work constantly with other people, reporting in to superiors who are directive and aggressive, the stress will get greater and greater. Stress levels will peak for INFPs if work politics require that they conform to an inimical set of values.

It is quite common for the Dominant function, in this case Introverted Feeling, to become more and more pronounced as stress levels increase. Any criticism will tend to be taken personally and Sensing data will often be ignored unless it reinforces the feeling of hurt. As INFPs get more and more touchy, their normal easygoing nature becomes less and less apparent until the 'flip' into Extraverted Thinking occurs. INFPs will then become coldly critical, very pernickety, and erupt in harshly critical observations about the emotional demands people are making on them or in pointing out others' shortcomings.

INFPs will also be overly sensitive to the possibility of their own incompetence. The untutored Extraverted Thinking function will cause the INFP to be coldly rational and even combative. There may also be a strong desire to rush into action to correct an imagined fault. This may take the form of the INFP assuming an authoritarian role and issuing commands right, left and centre.

Once the INFP is in the grip of his or her Inferior Extraverted Thinking function, it may be possible just to wait it out until the storm blows over. If not, a friend or colleague may be able to encourage the INFP's Tertiary Sensing function to make a deliberate effort to get some hard evidence that the situation is not as dire as the INFP has reasoned it to be. Having once ceased to be driven by the critical logic and reason of the Extraverted Thinking function, the INFP's Auxiliary Extraverted iNtuition function can be encouraged to affirm the INFP as to his or her own worth in the context of the big picture.

Life-giving strategies

INFPs tend to be highly selective about the information they gather from the outer world, filtering it so that only what supports their own ideas and values is recognized. This can lead to a certain self-centredness, and some conscious development of their Extraverted iNtuition function will be beneficial, acquiring information non-selectively.

Developing their ability to share more of what is going on inside themselves will help INFPs become less insular, as will canvassing the opinions of others in the process of making a decision. With their tight focus on the present, learning to look ahead, trying to acquire some sensory data that helps them understand the world around them and how they are really viewed by others, INFPs will become easier to live and work with. This will be easier if the INFP can find a trusted colleague who has a natural affinity for data gathering using his or her senses. Having said that, INFPs will benefit from becoming consciously aware of their inclination towards being too trusting.

INFPs will benefit from using their Thinking function to analyse the information they have gathered with their iNtuition function, instead of evaluating it solely on its consistency with their own value system. Similarly, learning to complete a task or project before embarking on the next because it is more interesting will be beneficial.

Summary

The gentle, flexible, idealistic and perfectionist INFP is a sensitive and caring listener whose reticence and tolerance can unexpectedly turn to adamancy when his or her internal values are compromised. As democratic leaders INFPs' creativity and personal example will set the tone for those they lead, whom they will praise and affirm. Because they have a very firm idea of how things should be, INFPs should be aware of the possibility of being perceived as coercive. Likely to have only a few, really close friends, INFPs continually strive for self-improvement. INFPs will benefit from developing their pragmatism and activism and from learning that constructive negative feedback can be just as helpful as praise and affirmation in growing and developing others.

11

Introducing the ENFP leader – the Imaginative Motivator

Dominant Extraverted iNtuition with Introverted Feeling

————•◆•————

ENFPs are warm, energetic and enthusiastic seekers after personal authenticity who are stimulated to mental creativity by the outer world. Committed to living out their internally held values, ENFPs find meaning in everything and see patterns and possibilities, especially in the people they serve.

* * *

Introduction

ENFPs can turn their hand to almost anything and may have several careers in the course of their lives. They are guided by their internal value system and driven to live out those values so they can be assured they are being true to themselves. ENFPs are very gifted at dealing with people, with a genuine warm interest in others, and have a strong need to be liked. They are insightful about the needs and aspirations of those they serve and have a rare talent for bringing out the best in them.

Type dynamics tell us that ENFPs have a Dominant function of Extraverted iNtuition that sees exciting potential in other people and enthusiastically helps to develop it. The Auxiliary function of Introverted Feeling continually references the internal value system to evaluate and organize the ENFP's approach to that development process. The Tertiary function of Extraverted Thinking applies logic and reason to the various developmental possibilities on offer and the Inferior function of Introverted Sensing stores and retrieves details and facts about people who matter.

The four functions are used in four steps, one after the other – Dominant, Auxiliary, Tertiary and Inferior – but it is an unconscious, and very fast, process. The Tertiary and Inferior functions may be used minimally or not at all. If used, they may be less well executed, or even omitted altogether, if they have undergone little or no development. So when approaching a problem to solve, ENFPs assimilate all sorts of information and impressions about the presenting situation, focusing on the people involved, and generate lots of different ways their lives could be enhanced (Extraverted iNtuition). These various possibilities will then be checked out against the ENFP's internal value system to ensure that none of the options will violate those values (Introverted Feeling). Logic and reason will then be brought to bear on the remaining options (Thinking) before the ENFP's internal database is accessed to find any similar previous situations that have a bearing on the current one, and details of the current situation will be stored (Introverted Sensing).

The top priority of ENFPs is to pursue the process of self-actualization – 'I exist, therefore I must become.' They value authenticity and integrity, their own identity, their uniqueness as a person and the uniqueness of those they serve. They have a strong sense of justice but that will be subservient to harmony with their own internal value system. Naturally intuitive about the needs and aspirations of others, ENFPs are finely attuned to the possibilities of people and institutions, and are positive and encouraging in pursuing them.

Characteristically innovative and empathetic, ENFPs call forth the possibilities in others but can become overinvolved in the emotional undercurrents of a situation and find it hard to say 'no'. ENFPs have a rebellious streak, with a tendency to have difficulty with authoritative structures and authority figures and, given the choice, would side with their peers over and against authority. This may in part be linked to the ENFP's tendency to view his or her own values as the only possible ones.

In a team context, ENFPs are the glue that sticks the team together. Often highly entertaining, ENFPs will be the ones to plunge into awkward moments and make a jocular remark or voice what everybody else is feeling. Their engaging enthusiasm will encourage the other members of the team to mix in and pull together but they do have an unfortunate tendency to be underprepared, in the – often unjustified – assurance that they can wing it. There is a danger that ENFPs may be viewed as too shallow and flippant ever to be taken seriously, especially if they are unsure they are liked and may be working just that bit too hard to be accepted.

ENFPs can be relied on to find whatever fun is to be had in a situation and will always be encouraging the other members of the team to recognize and value one another's strengths. This focus on fun can be at the expense of completing the task in hand. ENFPs will typically relish a prospective major change, bringing their enthusiasm, spontaneity and flexibility to the party and eagerly anticipating the new. If involved with identifying possibilities and generating options, the ENFP Perceiving preference can lead to an inability to reach a stopping point and draw this stage to a close.

As leaders ENFPs will strive to create an atmosphere of trust and openness and will be very clear about the roles they expect those they lead to undertake. They will lead by example, empowering their people and nurturing the belief that anything is possible. They will always give credit where it is due and their style will be warm, personal and affirming. ENFPs give every impression of being democratic but they tend to know exactly where the enterprise – which comprises the people – should be going, and exactly how to get the people to go there, so there can be a feeling of being coerced by an ENFP leader.

Comfort zone

The Dominant Extraverted iNtuition function combined with the Auxiliary Introverted Feeling function strongly inclines ENFPs towards the area of pastoral care. When they are with somebody, ENFPs have an instinctive feel for what that person has the potential to be, and they are committed to bringing that about if at all possible. The Extraversion preference means that ENFPs get their energy from being with people, so pastoral visiting is likely to figure large in the ENFP's ministry. Meeting new people in the parish, and ensuring they see those whom they intuitively know have emotional needs will also be energizing.

ENFPs strive to bring harmony with their own internal value system into any parish situation and they will be adept at providing emotional support for those in their care. They will find it highly rewarding to be involved in the emotional problems of those among whom they minister, and the need to develop the potential of the members of the congregation and parish will be paramount for ENFPs. They will not feel a great drive for social action, rather they will be focused on the possibilities and opportunities for their people. ENFPs are catalysts for change but their lodestone will always be the emotional needs of their people and harmony with their own internal values.

This focus on the emotional needs of others will be particularly true of the occasional offices of baptism, marriage and funerals. The opportunities for nurturing spiritual growth in baptism families and wedding couples will be seized with joy, as will those for pastoral care in the preparation, conduct and follow-up of a funeral service. ENFPs will need to have a strategy for handing on these families to other people, particularly those needing bereavement support.

ENFPs are happy in the world of people possibilities and opportunities. The development of a new parish vision, mission statement and strategic goals will be comfortable for ENFPs. Developing and exploring lots of different possible futures for the members of the congregation and for the people in the parish, and finding many and varied implementation possibilities, will all be hugely energizing for ENFPs. The problem will be knowing when to stop.

ENFPs will prefer spontaneous, open-ended, visionary worship that is both relational and vocal and includes periods of silence. Leading worship, especially with large congregations, will tend to be energizing for ENFPs, and the opportunities for fellowship before, during and after the service will make worship times highly congenial. Equally, the people aspects of running meetings, and the opportunities for fellowship, will appeal to the ENFP's Feeling preference; but the need for structure and the focus on facts and details required by most parish business meetings will be trying for the ENFP's Dominant Perceiving preference, iNtuition.

The preparation of sermons or courses that articulate and draw out the hard questions of faith as they relate to people, possibly finding innovative ways of looking at them, will appeal to ENFPs' Introverted iNtuition preference. Finding fresh gospel truths will be a joy, as will posing questions for their congregations to dwell on. Time spent alone in the study will tend to be draining for the Extraverted ENFP, but as the material being prepared will be personal and orientated towards the people implications of living out a Christian faith, this may well be offset by the energy gained from having been with the people for whom the material is intended.

Prayer for Extravert ENFPs will preferably be in a group or some form of communal prayer. God is likely to be encountered in the outer world, in and through people, an immanent, accessible God personally inspiring and energizing his creatures. The Extraversion preference will often mean that ENFP insights and thoughts will not be fully formed until they have been talked through with other people. The prayer of the iNtuitive is varied, creative, mystical and filled with future possibilities – the journey towards becoming the people that God has created us to be. Symbology is important, hinting at awe and wonder and bringing a sense of the numinous. The Extraverted Feeling preference needs harmonious interrelationship with others, and that is where God will be found. Silence will be important – it will allow ENFPs to dwell on the wonder of relationship with God and with others. The personal value system of individuals with a Feeling preference will be a significant part of their spirituality. ENFPs are most likely to grow spiritually in an environment in which people are actively and overtly valued.

Outside comfort zone

The focus on detail and the nitty-gritty practicalities of fabric maintenance will be draining for ENFPs, as will the step-by-step requirements of a church re-ordering process. With their Perceiving preference for going with the flow and leaving everything open, the everyday detail of good administration will be hard for ENFPs – they will always prefer to be out and about, responding to the needs of others.

With their Auxiliary Introverted Feeling function driving their need for harmony with their internal values, ENFPs dislike conflict with those who matter to them and will go some way to avoid it. Difficult pastoral situations that require tough decisions, mediation that requires dispassionate rationality or thinking through the ramifications of the alternatives available (requiring the use of their Tertiary Thinking), will be stressful for ENFPs.

Stress response

ENFPs work best in an environment that recognizes and encourages their innovative people development skills and their passion for all things new – and where the implementation of these great new ideas can be left to somebody else. Ideally ENFPs will not be restricted by petty rules and regulations or by having to conform to 'the way we do things round here'. They will work best surrounded by others who are willing to innovate, preferably people who are expert in their own fields and who can work independently. ENFPs need recognition for their creativity and originality and can work on a number of things simultaneously.

Because they welcome and embrace the future, ENFPs are at their best in fast-moving, rapidly changing environments. Stimulated and challenged by seemingly intractable problems, ENFPs work best when left to their own devices, exploring new possibilities. Competitive and ambitious, they are fed by recognition and reward for what they achieve and are happiest in work environments that appreciate them for being resourceful in pursuing a variety of interests with little or no need of supervision. Flexible, varied, rapidly changing environments suit ENFPs down to the ground. Engaging and sociable, they are happy to encourage others to join them in their enthusiastic pursuit of their goals.

Work will begin to become stressful when rules and regulations bring predictability and constraint and the achievement of assigned tasks is monitored and measured. Where work is not intellectually challenging, where supervisors are hidebound and closed to new ideas, where independence of thought and action is discouraged and where significant amounts of detail are required, this will cause ENFPs increasing levels of stress. If the work environment begins to violate the ENFP's deeply held values, for example with the arrival of a new bishop with a very different approach from his predecessor, this will be very stressful.

Stress levels will continue to increase if ENFPs are required to constrain their creative thinking or if their intellectual competence is called into question. Having to work with too many details under close supervision, especially if it is incompetent, will be a nightmare for ENFPs. Signs that the stress is getting to them often involve ENFPs taking on more and more work, becoming argumentative or passive aggressive and less and less effective.

A number of factors – fatigue and physical exhaustion, especially if caused by taking on too much, eating and sleeping too little – may cause ENFPs to trigger their Inferior function and result in the body reacting by developing a physical illness. Too much detailed work over an extended period can cause a similar reaction, especially if it entails battling the bureaucrats.

It is reasonably common for individuals to exaggerate their Dominant function just before they fall into the grip of the Inferior function. For an ENFP this would probably look like the development of a plethora of ideas and possibilities, none of which had been subjected to the usual examination through the lens of the internal value system. As this lopsidedness becomes less and less effective, the usual energy and enthusiasm ENFPs have for their work deteriorates into gloom and despondency.

The ENFP's 'flip' into his or her Inferior function of Introverted Sensing often presents as an obsessive concentration on irrelevant details, with all big-picture perspective lost. This focus on internal processing is unnatural and uncomfortable for ENFPs, so energy drains away and they can become withdrawn and depressed, convinced they are not and never have been lovable. This may lead to an unhealthy focus on the state of their own physical health – ENFPs can become acutely aware of their own bodies and may imagine they are developing all sorts of physical symptoms. Obsessive surfing of medical advice sites on the internet can feed this tendency to hypochondria, and only the direst of possible explanations will be deemed correct.

If one likens life to a game of Snakes and Ladders, the experience of descending into the grip of the Inferior function can feel like landing on the head of the longest snake and ending up virtually back at the start. As with the board game, it is highly unusual to land immediately on the bottom rung of the ladder that takes you back to where you came from. A solution that often works is to take the smallest ladder available, represented by the Tertiary function; ENFPs have a Tertiary function of Thinking. It is highly unlikely that one can make this journey by one's own efforts, so ENFPs need a trusted friend or colleague, adept at using their own Thinking function, to help in the process of recovery.

ENFPs can be helped to become aware that their current actions are illogical and unreasonable given the actual situation. Once that is recognized, ENFPs can be encouraged to take sufficient rest, to respond to their bodily needs in a gentle, restorative way, perhaps coupled with some mild physical exercise. Refusing to take on any more tasks and rigorously prioritizing and/or delegating current tasks can begin to relieve some of the pressure. With returning physical health and a lessening of the pressures of task completion, ENFPs can bring the analytical perspective of their Tertiary Extraverted Thinking to bear, shining the light of logic and reason on the irrational state in which they have been. Once that has been accomplished, normal service can be resumed.

Life-giving strategies

ENFPs tend to leap off in the direction of the next exciting possibility or opportunity, especially if it looks better than the status quo; they would benefit from accepting that just because the grass is on the other side of the fence, it is not *necessarily* greener. Even though it may be uncomfortable to use their Inferior Sensing function, it would be helpful for ENFPs to learn the discipline of consciously considering the facts before making a decision. Also, developing the self-discipline to complete one task before leaping off into another would pay dividends.

ENFPs would do well to build some regular physical exercise into their daily routine, to be gentle with themselves and to learn to listen to their bodies. It is hoped that ENFPs who are in Christian ministry will have a regular prayer discipline, but this may benefit from being further developed along more meditational lines.

ENFPs would do well to temper their enthusiasm for some of their wilder inspirations with the thought that they may actually need some more polishing before they are ready to roll. Also, developing their skills of active listening would help ENFPs to become more aware that those who counsel caution may have a point. When the advice is of the look before you leap variety, those offering the advice may well have experienced the gorse bush on the other side of the wall, so they may be offering constructive advice and not just being annoying killjoys. In addition, learning that those who offer constructive criticism are not always making direct personal attacks would bring more equilibrium to the ENFP's life.

Summary

ENFPs are warm, flexible, adaptable, open, people-orientated types who are gifted at understanding the potential of others and who bring energy and enthusiasm to the enterprise of realizing it. They are good starters but poor finishers who are rooted in the present. They intuitively collect all sorts of interesting titbits about those they serve from the outer world and weave them into new and fascinating possibilities. Engaging, caring and empathetic, ENFPs need to be aware that their warm, collegial informality may be perceived as overfamiliarity.

12

Introducing the ENFJ leader – the Compassionate Facilitator

Dominant Extraverted Feeling with Introverted iNtuition

———•◆•———

ENFJs care deeply about other people and want to make their lives better. They are focused on the possibilities in others, and their outstanding people skills help them to understand, support and grow those they serve.

* * *

Introduction

The phrase 'You are all heart' describes the ENFJ to a tee. They are definitively the 'people people' of the type world, inhabiting a world of people possibilities. They have an intuitive understanding of the emotional needs and aspirations of those they meet, and have a rare talent for drawing out the best in others. Offering love, emotional support and hospitality are hallmarks of the ENFJ.

Type dynamics tell us that ENFJs have a Dominant function of Extraverted Feeling that leads ENFJs to place a high value on the groups to which they belong and emphasizes the importance of harmony within that group, with ENFJs developing structures that energize people and allow the groups of which they are part to flourish. The Auxiliary function of Introverted iNtuition helps the ENFJ to understand instinctively the emotional needs and aspirations of others and to develop new and different ways for people and groups to realize their potential. The Tertiary Extraverted Sensing function brings options that are immediate and practical into the equation and the Inferior function of Introverted Thinking uses logic and reason to evaluate personal interactions.

The four functions are used in four steps, one after the other – Dominant, Auxiliary, Tertiary and Inferior – but it is an unconscious, and very fast, process. The Tertiary and Inferior functions may be used minimally or not at all. If used, they may be less well executed, or even omitted altogether, if they have undergone little or no development. So for problem-solving, ENFJs will first and foremost place everything in the context of group harmony and explore how the presenting situation affects people (Extraverted Feeling). More information will be drawn 'from the ether', mostly subconsciously (gestures, body language, tone of voice), to determine the emotional needs of those the ENFJs are with (Introverted iNtuition). Further data will be gathered through the five senses before logic and reason are applied to test the possible solutions that have been developed.

ENFJs present as open, friendly, caring and compassionate but one would do well to be aware that there is a tungsten core. They are highly skilled persuaders who are past masters at building consensus, even when there is a wide range of opinions. With their deep understanding of people and what makes them tick, ENFJs are able to get others to do almost anything; there is always a danger that they can be perceived as coercive.

ENFJs tend to be more reserved than other Extraverted types and can be very reticent about sharing their own views or beliefs, often because doing so might hamper the harmony of the group or the development of others. Often acting as catalysts for change, ENFJs see many possibilities for the future but are always looking for the best in others, which they typically do with great insight.

In a team environment, ENFJs focus on the common good. They will typically tune in to the other members of the team, getting to know the opinion of each member, then work to build consensus by drawing out possibilities that encompass as many of these opinions as possible and then cooperatively develop the way forward. However, they can be guilty of focusing too much on human issues and of not voicing dissent if, in doing so, they might have a negative impact on the loyalty of the team or the harmony of the group. ENFJs typically have great personal warmth and are very sensitive to the different needs of the team members, whom they nurture and encourage by affirming each individual's contribution. ENFJs are a priceless resource in times of change as they are the ones who will be emotionally supportive to those having difficulty with the change.

As leaders ENFJs will develop an organizational structure that plays to the strengths of the members of the team, then provide overall direction that encourages collaboration and individual contributions. They will typically enjoy leading teams and will focus on the growth of both the individuals and the organization, with much positive affirmation; and the teams they lead can be highly motivated and very productive.

Comfort zone

The Dominant Extraverted Feeling function gives ENFJs a natural care and compassion that helps to make them among the most gifted of the types in the area of pastoral care. They have an instinctive gift of timing that helps them know when the moment is right for a telephone call or a visit. The Extraversion preference means that ENFJs get their energy from being with people, so pastoral visiting is likely to figure large in the ENFJ's ministry. Meeting new people in the parish and ensuring they see those whom they intuitively know have emotional needs will also be energizing.

ENFJs strive to bring harmony to any parish situation and will be adept at providing emotional support for those in their care. ENFJs will find it highly rewarding to be involved in the emotional problems of those among whom they minister, and the needs of the members of the congregation and parish will be paramount for ENFJs, in some cases even overriding issues of right and wrong. ENFJs will not feel a great drive for social action, rather they will be focused on the emotional needs and aspirations of their people. ENFJs are catalysts for change but their lodestone will always be the potentialities of their people and harmony with their own internal values.

This focus on the emotional needs of others will be particularly true of the occasional offices of baptism, marriage and funerals. The opportunities for nurturing spiritual growth in baptism families and wedding couples will be seized with joy, as will those for pastoral care in the preparation, conduct and follow-up of a funeral service. ENFJs will need to have a strategy for handing on these families to other people, particularly those needing bereavement support.

The Extraversion preference will incline ENFJs towards worship styles that are relational and vocal; their iNtuition preference will want visions and future possibilities to be articulated; their Feeling preference will respond to periods of silence and their judging preference will incline them towards structured and controlled forms of worship, so formal liturgies will be appealing. Leading worship, especially for large congregations, will be energizing, given ENFJs' Extraversion preference – their Dominant Extraverted Feeling function will incline them to meld the congregation together into a harmonious worshipping community. Opportunities for social interaction and fellowship as part of the worship experience will also be highly congenial to ENFJs.

The preparation of sermons or courses that articulate and draw out the hard questions of faith as they relate to people, possibly finding innovative ways of looking at them, will appeal to ENFJs' Introverted iNtuition preference. Finding fresh gospel truths will be a joy, as will posing questions for congregations to dwell on. Time spent alone in the study will tend to be draining for the Extraverted ENFJ, but as the material being prepared will be personal and orientated towards the people implications of living out a Christian faith, this may well be offset by the energy gained from having been with the people for whom the material is intended.

Prayer for Extravert ENFJs will preferably be in a group or will be some form of communal prayer. God is likely to be encountered in the outer world, in and through people, an immanent, accessible God personally inspiring and energizing his creatures. The Extraversion preference will often mean that ENFJ insights and thoughts will not be fully formed until they have been talked through with other people. The prayer of the Introverted iNtuitive is varied, creative, mystical, private and filled with future possibilities – the journey towards becoming the people God has created us to be. Symbology is important, hinting at awe and wonder and bringing a sense of the numinous. The Extraverted Feeling preference needs harmonious interrelationship with others, and that is where God will be found. Silence will be important – it will allow ENFJs to dwell on the wonder of relationship with God and with others. The personal value system of individuals with a Feeling preference will be a significant part of their spirituality. ENFJs are most likely to grow spiritually in an environment in which people are actively and overtly valued.

The iNtuition preference of ENFJs will make them future-orientated, so the development of a parish vision, mission and strategic goals will be very much to their taste. Their Judging preference will incline them towards detailed planning and sticking to a schedule but, again, the Extraverted Feeling preference will always make these subservient to the needs of the flock. Meetings will be grasped as opportunities for fellowship and service, and will tend to be energizing for Extraverted ENFJs. Everyday business meetings focused on the details of the present will be less congenial, whereas future-focused planning meetings will be welcomed.

Outside comfort zone

The focus on detail and the nitty-gritty practicalities of fabric maintenance will be draining for ENFJs, as will the step-by-step requirements of a church re-ordering process. Despite their Judging preference for order and control, the everyday detail of good administration will be hard for ENFJs – they will always prefer to be out and about, responding to the needs of others.

Following through from a vision of what might be possible to the practicality of a social-action project would be unusual for ENFJs; they would much prefer to leave the doing to others.

With their Dominant Extraverted Feeling function driving their need for harmony, ENFJs dislike conflict and will go some way to avoid it. Difficult pastoral situations that require tough decisions, mediation that requires dispassionate rationality or thinking through the ramifications of the alternatives available – requiring the use of their Inferior Introverted Thinking – will be stressful for ENFJs.

ENFJs are susceptible to the temptation to become control freaks, so unplanned situations, uncontrolled spontaneity in worship or disturbances in routine will be stressful for the ENFJ's Judging preference. Some rigidity of attitude may be exhibited by ENFJs if a suggestion or proposal is made that does not fit with their view of the world and how it should be – particularly if the benefits of the proposal do not accrue to the people the ENFJ considers deserving.

Stress response

ENFJs work best in an environment that allows them to live out their core values – one that is focused on altruism rather than profit and on making the world a better place. The contribution ENFJs want to make to society at large and to individuals and groups in particular will ideally be one that has little or no petty bureaucracy and allows, and celebrates, social interaction.

ENFJs are happy to accept responsibility and will be highly motivated to pursue the goals of the organization they work for, provided those goals are in line with their own values and principles. A variety of tasks within a clear reporting structure, with the opportunity for independent working, will be energizing. The key element of any working environment for ENFJs, however, is the people with whom they will want to feel connected and in tune. With their Dominant Extraverted Feeling function giving them a sharp focus on group harmony, ENFJs value others, and need to feel valued themselves, to give of their best. Recognition of their own individual contribution to the overall enterprise will be affirming and motivational for ENFJs; conversely, its absence will have a negative effect. Actively negative feedback may well be taken very personally by ENFJs.

Work will begin to become stressful if there is tension, conflict and interpersonal competition in the workplace. Equally, pressure on time that prevents ENFJs from doing as good a job as they would like to will be perceived as stressful. Lack of control, task overload and additional tasks assigned at the last minute will be very stressful. With their need to care for their own families, ENFJs may also perceive stress in their work–life balance.

If and when stress rises to unacceptable levels, ENFJs may exaggerate their Dominant Extraverted Feeling function and try to impose harmony and good feeling on their colleagues even if it is unwelcome. The inevitable negative response to this leads to ENFJs swapping their characteristic focus on people, their general optimism and their enthusiasm for the task at hand for a withdrawn, listless pessimism and resigned martyrdom. If they 'flip' into the Inferior Introverted Thinking function, ENFJs can become highly critical, bossy and overbearing. Unconcerned about the emotional effect it will have, ENFJs can become aggressive, spiteful and coldly cutting. All too soon this negativity turns inwards, and ENFJs can become depressed and withdrawn and see no good in themselves whatever.

With their Tertiary Sensing function unlikely to give ENFJs accurate data with which to work, the Inferior Introverted Thinking function may develop logical analyses that are erroneous, make conspiracy theories seem persuasive and promote rigid and idiosyncratic thinking. There may also be an obsessional seeking after absolute truth, scouring the shelves of bookshops for self-help books that promise to give the reader the answer. While ENFJs would normally be the ones to be convening and running support groups, in the grip of their Inferior Introverted Thinking function they may well find solace in attending such groups and being assured that others are suffering a similar fate.

One way out of a 'grip' experience is to be encouraged to use the Tertiary function. ENFJs may find that solitary study time, or the discipline of writing a journal – both Sensing activities – may help them get back in touch with their Feeling function. Similarly, talking through the issues with a third party, coming to understand that they cannot always improve people or enforce group harmony, and involving themselves in a new venture, may help ENFJs back to equilibrium.

Life-giving strategies

ENFJs will benefit from developing their less preferred functions of Sensing and Thinking; learning that a less emotionally based, more task-focused approach to the job can be equally supportive of the people with whom they work, as can genuinely delegating responsibility and allowing others to make their own mistakes. Group harmony is ideal for ENFJs, certainly, but it does not mean that good cannot come from a slightly more abrasive atmosphere – it is the grit that stimulates the development of the pearl. Equally, learning to take constructive criticism less personally, and trying to understand that personal improvement can come from accepting and responding to such criticism, can bring positive benefits.

ENFJs are expert at empathy and therefore can immerse themselves in the emotional maelstrom of others. While this can be immensely affirming and may feed the ENFJ's need to help others, it can be emotionally draining if time out is not deliberately sought. Allowing themselves to plan-in periods of free time when there is no expectation of performance, and having a close friend to 'dump' on, can help ENFJs to relax and just be.

ENFJs tend to know that they are right, so giving careful consideration to opinions that may challenge that view, and taking a more dispassionate, rational look at a pet theory by seeking some hard evidence to allow that to happen, will be beneficial. Refraining from always seeking closure, and allowing things to hang loose, may reduce the pressure to succeed.

Summary

The charming, warm-hearted, hospitable and gracious ENFJs are finely tuned to the emotional needs and aspirations of others, are highly gifted in their ability to discern the potential of an individual, group or institution and are motivated to bring it about. They need to be aware of their tendency so to sublimate their own needs to the needs of others that they may do themselves a disservice. They also need to be aware that they may have such a burning conviction about what is right for somebody that there is a real danger of their being coercive. Nurturing and affirming leaders, ENFJs will benefit from coming to understand that unswerving loyalty may not always be justified and that negative feedback is not necessarily personal and destructive.

13

Introducing the INTJ leader – the Conceptual Planner

Dominant Introverted iNtuition with Extraverted Thinking

———◆◆◆———

INTJs are characterized by their inner energy, their restlessness and their commitment to improvement. They are hard to know well and their air of critical detachment can cause others to assume that the INTJ is both arrogant and aloof.

* * *

Introduction

This independent type might be characterized as the swan; calm, serene, unflappable, capable – often so much so as to be seen as something of an enigma and rather intimidating and unapproachable. INTJs are energized by their own inner world (Introversion), have a preference for acquiring information by using their sixth sense rather than the other five (iNtuition) and have a preference for processing that information, and coming to decisions, using logic and reason (Thinking). This type prefers to reach closure by coming to a decision rather than leaving things open and unresolved (Judging).

INTJs will see themselves as always in need of improvement – there will always be some fine tuning to be done, in any aspect of life, and any playtime will be approached with serious, almost work-like, intent. The most stressful thing for INTJs is to be incompetent at something – usually they will not do anything at which they are not good or very good.

The type dynamics of the INTJ show that the Dominant Function is Introverted iNtuition, the Auxiliary Function is Extraverted Thinking, the Tertiary function is Introverted Feeling and the Inferior Function is Extraverted Sensing.

The four functions are used in four steps, one after the other – Dominant, Auxiliary, Tertiary and Inferior – but it is an unconscious, and very fast, process. The Tertiary and Inferior functions may be used minimally or not at all. If used, they may be less well executed, or even omitted altogether, if they have undergone little or no development. Faced with a situation, then, the INTJ's first response will be to look at the big picture – think how it fits into their mental map of the world and see any future possibilities (iNtuition). Then they will apply logic to the situation – 'What is a rational response to this?' (Thinking) – before considering the impact on their own values and how other people might be affected (Feeling). The last response will be to look at the facts – to get some details about the situation (Sensing).

In a team environment the INTJ persuades co-workers with clear thinking, rational argument, logic and observational detail; it is possible to assume that the step-by-step approach of the INTJ indicates someone with a Sensing preference. The province of the INTJ is new ideas, so major contributions to the team endeavour will be made by suggesting new perspectives or insights. The ability to build on the ideas of others, possibly taking a number of different ideas and synthesizing them into new solutions, is a great strength.

As a leader the INTJ is able to conceive and articulate a compelling vision of the future and to keep the team on message by clearly setting out goals and expected results. If there is a need for hard words to rectify poor performance, the INTJ will be up to the task. The INTJ needs to be aware of the

tendency to accept good performance as the norm and consequently not to affirm, praise and appreciate others sufficiently.

Comfort zone

With a rich inner life (Introverted iNtuition), the INTJ will be
nourished by vision and new ideas – the big picture, what the
future holds. The development of a parish vision statement,
re-thinking the mission statement and strategic planning will
all be meat and drink to the INTJ.

The Introverted INTJ will be energized and refreshed by
spending time alone – either in prayer or reading and writing
in the study. The INTJ's Introverted iNtuition will relish
imaginative prayer styles such as the Ignatian practice of
placing oneself inside a Gospel story and encountering Jesus.
Unexplained symbology, intriguing sculptures, abstract pictures –
these will all feed the iNtuitive preference. When I was at
theological college, one of my elective modules was Spirituality.
I chose to focus on the MBTI® and spirituality, and was lucky
enough to be able to talk through aspects of my work with
one of our regular visitors, Sister Deirdre Michael CSMV, a
very experienced spiritual director and MBTI retreat leader. In
the course of one conversation, she asserted that 'the Inferior
function is the undefended wicket-gate through which God
can get'. As the INTJ's Inferior function is Sensing, a prayer
style that engages all the senses can be truly rich – for example,
the classic Taizé candlelit service of Prayers Around the Cross,
with incense burning, biblical phrases sung over and over
again in four-part harmony, a piece of recorded music, an
artefact to handle, possibly even bread to share and a period
of silence.

The iNtuitive INTJ will resonate strongly with the words
used in the licensing of a new Anglican ministry – 'the Church
is called to proclaim afresh [the gospel] in each generation'

(from the Declaration of Assent in the Church of England Licensing Service). The idea of finding fresh insights into the gospel message or finding new ways of doing things in the church will excite the INTJ. When someone says 'If it ain't broke, don't fix it', the INTJ response will often be 'Even if it ain't broke, let's fix it anyway.' Similar energy will encourage the INTJ in theological questions – finding answers to questions of faith that others find difficult. Indeed, INTJs may raise them themselves. The combination of iNtuition and Thinking will often allow INTJs to get a 'helicopter view' of an issue or problem; they will then be able to articulate that overarching view in a way that may be helpful. For some, however, the intensely conceptual nature of most of the INTJs' thinking will be very difficult.

With the iNtuitive's love of new ideas, change will usually be relished. Often seeing change as yet another new challenge, INTJs will be happiest when they can influence the change envisaged. Designing a change management process will appeal to the INTJ, but as in all aspects of life, the INTJ needs to beware of the details or of spending too much time on tasks that are pure routine. There is always a danger of the INTJ overlooking important details or getting bored when things are too much the same.

The Thinking preference, combined with the visionary orientation of the iNtuitive, will make the INTJ happiest when creating a challenging framework for the future of the parish, sector or area of responsibility. Because they will always be seeking to improve themselves, INTJs will be keen to develop others, especially if they are responsible for training more junior clergy. While this may take the form of coaching, the INTJ will be more comfortable with mentoring – the non-directive approach of the coach will be difficult for an INTJ to maintain. The INTJ's Thinking function will occasionally lead to somewhat insensitive handling of performance that is less than excellent – indeed, the INTJ may be experienced as unreasonably critical and demanding. It has to be said, however, that INTJs demand no less of themselves.

The INTJ's Judging orientation prefers order and structure, so leading worship in the context of a familiar liturgy will typically be done outstandingly well. The combination of iNtuition with Thinking will lead to preaching that tends to be inspirational and visionary – logically constructed sermons that paint a big picture of how things might be. Often these will be concluded with a challenge to some form of self-improvement – or at least openness to God's transforming power – often in the form of a question. The preference for Introversion will often mean that this essentially Extraverted activity will be emotionally draining – a significant amount of emotional energy will have been expended in leading public worship and preaching, so there will usually be a need for the INTJ to have a time of rest and quiet after a morning's services. Teaching and training, either within the parish context or extracurricularly, will also be strengths. Leading small groups will be intellectually satisfying for INTJs, but given their constant striving for improvement, always with the caveat that they should not expect too much of the group's members.

While meetings will be draining in a similar way to leading worship, chairing meetings such as the parochial church council or the annual parochial church meeting will be comfortable for the INTJ. The Judging orientation will be at home with the order and structure of the agenda, the Thinking function will be able to meet and handle issues objectively and rationally as they arise during the meeting, and the iNtuiting function will be able to hear the music as well as the words in the interplay between those attending the meeting. This will allow opportunities for enabling and facilitating the contributions of the more reticent and the avoidance of too many excursions into territory more properly the concern of another forum –

particularly where there is a tendency to repeat work already done at an inappropriate level of detail.

The INTJ's Judging preference will need plans and schedules for comfort. Worship services should start on time and should follow the planned structure (although the iNtuitive preference may have planned-in something just a little different this week). The INTJ will often need the reassurance of a to-do list – sometimes writing down tasks that have already been completed that day, just so they can be crossed off. What a sense of achievement that brings.

Outside comfort zone

The Introversion preference of INTJs indicates that they will not relish contact with people – it will drain rather than energize them. The classic model of the visiting vicar – dropping in for a cuppa and a chat, seeking out new people, being out and about in the parish – will not suit the INTJ. However, pastoral visiting with a purpose – visiting the sick or bereaved, a baptism family or a wedding couple – will be bearable; off-the-cuff dropping-in will not be the INTJ's style. The preference will always be to be at the desk, learning something new, preparing a sermon, mastering a new piece of technology.

The iNtuitive INTJ will find it difficult to engage with practical details. The church building's state of repair, the fine detail of a re-ordering or the minutiae of a quinquennial inspection will leave the INTJ cold. In fact it would be hazardous to leave such important elements to the INTJ minister because they will tend to be skipped over – or skimped on – as the INTJ's imagination soars on to the next big-picture possibility. A similar lesson can be learned about the routine of administration. It could be argued that the heart of the word 'administration' is 'ministry', so that it has an honoured and necessary place in the exercise of ordained ministry. INTJs will tend to employ a 'piling system' – they will know exactly in which of the many piles of paper in their study is the item being sought, and woe betide the one who tidies up the piles.

Those in ordained ministry are typically markedly conflict-averse and will go to great lengths to avoid confrontation with parishioners or colleagues. The INTJ's Thinking preference will tend to make INTJ ministers oblivious to the emotional under-currents in a pastoral situation. It will also, however, allow them to bring objective fairness and justice to bear. Hard decisions may also be easier for INTJs because the feelings of those involved will be less important to them than the logically correct decision with the least harmful consequences – seen in rational terms, of course.

While a harmonious atmosphere in the parish or congregation will naturally be more congenial, the INTJ will find it hard to do the wrong thing just to preserve harmony. As well as being seen as something of a cold fish, the INTJ can be experienced as insensitive and uncaring.

The INTJ's Judging preference will find going with the flow difficult. It has been said that there is no such thing as a mistake in liturgy, merely an alternative interpretation – very comforting for the inexperienced worship leader but, for the INTJ, not a licence for sloppiness. Variety, spontaneity and flexibility will appeal to the INTJ's iNtuitive preference but will cause his or her Judging preference a degree of stress.

Incompetence of any sort will always be anathema to the INTJ and may cause significant levels of stress.

Stress response

INTJs relish a work environment that is under their control both in terms of the methodology used and results achieved, where work can be scheduled flexibly and there is the greatest amount of autonomy. A clearly defined role and clearly defined boundaries and expectations will be energizing. An environment that is organized, well structured and with no surprises, with fellow team members who tell it like it is and where it is possible to get closure, will get the best from an INTJ.

Things will start to go awry if the INTJ is required to deal with significant amounts of detail, especially if it is in the outer world. Too much time in the outer world – being required to be Extraverted for extended periods – will begin to be stressful. Being required to work as a subordinate to people who are ignorant, illogical or irrational – or alongside fellow workers who leave things half done or whose performance leaves a lot to be desired – will cause increasing amounts of stress.

A work environment that is disorganized, crowded and noisy will be difficult for the INTJ. It has to be said that 'organized' does not necessarily mean tidy – it may mean that the 'piling' system previously alluded to is used as opposed to a filing system; the INTJ has a built-in mental tracking system that knows precisely where everything is. Another major stressor is being asked to compromise on personal high standards and principles or to be party to deceit or dishonesty.

One can tell when an INTJ is stressed – the 'flip' into the Inferior function occurs, and that Inferior function, Sensing, will take over. INTJs will tend to become completely absorbed in trivial detail – the fine detail of the layout of a document, getting to the next level in a computer game, the need to order books on a shelf by height – and ignore the major issue facing them. The usually fastidious INTJ may become sloppy and careless and, although never overly aware of the feelings of others, will tell it like it is in a curt and highly critical manner. It may become very important that a particular drawer in the filing cabinet be tidied up, or cleaning the PC screen may become paramount.

The classic INTJ stress response, however, is overindulgence in sensory pleasures. Bouts of hedonistic indulgence – eating too much, smoking, drinking heavily, watching too much television, recreational drug abuse – will inevitably be followed by feelings of self-loathing, which may trigger further such bouts to dull the pain.

Life-giving strategies

For INTJs to be more at peace with themselves and more in tune with those among whom they minister, they need to be more relaxed and open and less driven. If the Thinking function can be moderated – if the smile can be more in evidence than the frown, if help can be sought before the drama becomes a crisis, if feelings can be admitted to those who are close – the reputation for cold aloofness can be tempered.

In their dealings with others – fellow shepherds or flock – a less demanding approach will bear fruit. Finding the positive thing to say rather than the negative – praise rather than criticism – will be more acceptable to the recipients. If others can also be genuinely involved and consulted, especially where decisions or actions may affect them personally, this can nurture a very effective collaborative culture.

The need for constant improvement also needs to be reined in. Cultivating a fit-for-purpose attitude – 'Is this good *enough?*' – will relieve the pressure to perform. If the bar is constantly being raised – higher and higher standards being demanded – this can create an exhausting environment. Sometimes it might pay to postpone a decision – to go with the flow. Given the blind spot INTJs have about details, and their impatience with them, ensuring that someone who *is* good at detail has done the necessary preparatory work before a decision is taken may lead to better decisions in the long run.

With the INTJ's tendency for all play to be work, finding something to do for relaxation that does not entail learning a new skill or demand high levels of application and concentration will be life-enhancing.

Summary

The INTJ will exercise a ministry that is logical, ingenious, reflective, imaginative, rational, inventive, principled and fair. While constantly striving for self-improvement, the INTJ would do well to increase the ratio of praise to criticism, appreciating the need for detailed work to be done – and done by those more suited to it – before dreams can be realized. INTJs would do well to temper their need for closure by going with the flow occasionally, especially where a solution that is fit for purpose is acceptable instead of striving for the best possible solution. Raising the bar again and again is potentially a real hazard. Being aware of the impact of decisions on other people and involving them in the decision-making process would be good; as, indeed, would being open about their own feelings to those in their intimate circle. A smile would also not go amiss.

14

Introducing the INTP leader – the Objective Analyst

Dominant Introverted Thinking with Extraverted iNtuition

INTPs are natural logicians who like to concentrate on solving complex problems. Inclined towards the abstract, they strive for truth and precision and seek to create a logical internal model, based on rational principles, for understanding the world.

* * *

Introduction

Rodin may well have used an INTP as the model for his sculpture *The Thinker* – INTPs inhabit a world of conceptual possibilities, always striving to understand the world around them and to fit it all together to form a complete model. It would be interesting to know how many adherents of systematic theology are, or were, INTPs.

Type dynamics show that the INTP has a Dominant function of Introverted Thinking that organizes information logically into global systems that allow the world to be understood. The Auxiliary function is Extraverted iNtuition, so that information gathered and ideas generated are approached with curiosity and will often comprise internal pictures and patterns cast forward into the future. The Tertiary function of Introverted Sensing gives due weight to realities from the outer world and the Inferior function of Extraverted Feeling brings the needs and viewpoints of other people into the mix.

The four functions are used in four steps, one after the other – Dominant, Auxiliary, Tertiary and Inferior – but it is an unconscious, and very fast, process. The Tertiary and Inferior functions may be used minimally or not at all. If used, they may be less well executed, or even omitted altogether, if they have undergone little or no development. So in approaching problem-solving, INTPs will initially want to develop a logical framework within which the process can take place (Introverted Thinking). The continual data-gathering enterprise will correlate together impressions, nuances and possibilities and try to fit them into that logical framework (Extraverted iNtuition). Facts and details from the external world will then be sought to confirm and validate this newly enhanced model (Introverted Sensing). Finally, how potential decisions would impact on other people and on group harmony will be considered (Extraverted Feeling).

The Dominant Introverted Thinking function inclines INTPs to be enthusiastic visionaries who live almost entirely in their heads and work at a very conceptual level, producing highly complex ideas and thought forms. They tend to be independent, have little time for authoritarian structures or bureaucracies and will argue a case at the drop of a hat. They tend to present as shy and socially awkward, although among friends they can be very good company.

As a member of the team, INTPs will prefer to be in a loose federation of people as bright as themselves. It is highly unlikely that INTPs will be working in a subject area about which they know little, so they can be relied on to have a very good grasp of the subject matter, to act as a reference point for other members of the team, to be a dispassionate observer and listener who can then cut to the chase and articulate what the wood looks like without being distracted by the trees.

It is likely that the INTP will set out the principles on which the team will engage with its work, and will strive to develop a team culture that is flexible – but without any formal structure – and allows each individual to work independently. INTPs need to be aware of their tendency to be overly intellectual and very abstract, and aware of being perceived as unduly critical when they uncover drawbacks and mistakes in proposals that other team members put forward. With a very low tolerance of incompetence in themselves and others, INTPs may be guilty of focusing too much on accuracy and equity at the expense of the harmony of the team.

INTPs will approach a major change process analytically to develop an intellectual framework for the new order, but there may be little or no recognition of the human impact that the change may have. Used well in a team, INTPs can contribute greatly to the team endeavour with their analytical objectivity and intuitive grasp of implications and complications. They can usually generate a number of different solutions so that the team can decide together which way it wants to go. INTPs do, however, need to be aware of their tendency to abandon one task or project in favour of another more interesting one that arises.

As leaders INTPs will define and establish a set of ground rules, the following of which they will then work to encourage among those they lead. They will be little concerned with pre-defined roles and hierarchies and happiest affirming independence of thought and individual self-motivation in the members of their team. They will have little patience with team members who need to be closely supervised. INTPs will command loyalty and admiration with the quality of their ideas, and their inclination will always be to challenge the way things are. They are often prepared to take risks (always carefully calculated, of course), and will expect members of their team to act independently and will have little or no patience with those who do not.

Comfort zone

INTPs are only really happy when wrestling with intellectual challenges. They will relish the development of a finely argued sermon, often addressing a thorny problem in the life of faith. Always challenging the status quo, INTPs will relish raising issues of faith that others find intractable and will often want to question the orthodox position. Preaching and teaching will be a joy, but perhaps only for the one preaching or teaching rather than those hearing the sermon or lesson – INTPs have a tendency to traverse arcane reaches of abstract thought that may be accessible only to a university theology faculty. Sermons will usually be very challenging, and much food for thought will be offered for subsequent digestion. Teaching will be a pleasure if the students are intelligent, intellectually agile and able to argue well; more run-of-the-mill teaching, especially at a less rarefied intellectual level, will probably be viewed as a chore.

While they have little time for bureaucracy and day-to-day administration, INTPs do like to come up with innovative ways of doing things. New possibilities for ministry, developing the vision and mission of a church and conceiving overarching strategic goals will all be welcome grist to the INTP mill.

For individuals with a Thinking preference, the key measure in ministry will be effectiveness. Bringing objectivity to bear in crisis situations in ministry, the individual with the Thinking preference will pursue fairness and justice – being well liked will not be as important as finding a logical, reasoned solution. In taking difficult decisions in the parish, rational analysis that explores possible courses of action and their logical consequences will be the norm. Reasoned settlement of disputes with members of the staff team or of the congregation will be pursued.

The rich variety of parish ministry with its unpredictable occurrences, new and unplanned experiences and the real possibility of a break in routine will be very attractive to those with a Perceiving preference.

The Introverted pray-er is likely to prefer praying alone or in small groups. God is likely to be experienced as the 'still small voice' and as transcendent, unknowable and inaccessible. Silence and solitude will be preferred; too much noise or action will be very distracting.

The Thinking pray-er likes structure and dislikes repetition. Intelligibility will be important, as will the exercise of logic and reason. The search for truth and meaning will be a continual one, and God tends to be found in the mind and in experience. The doctrine of the church to which the thinker belongs will be important. Bible study will actually become prayer in the classical sense of reading and meditating on the word. Emotionalism in worship or prayer, or numinous religious experiences, will be thought suspect.

The preference for iNtuition will lead the INTP to prefer a varied, creative, mystical prayer style that opens up a number of possibilities and encourages intuitive leaps to find hidden meanings and connections. Symbology will be important, provided the symbols used are not explained. God will be experienced as a transcendent mystery that continually challenges the world to be the best that it can be. Formal prayer liturgies may get in the way of the INTP's wide-ranging questing.

Perceiving pray-ers need to beware of the possibility that they may never settle down to a particular style of prayer. This can be confusing as they are the most open to different paths and types of spiritual growth. God is a God of possibilities, pleasure and fun. Typically INTPs with a perceiving preference will find God in life through gathering experiences, insights, pleasures and relationships. They like to remain open to most possibilities and are comfortable with risk, ambiguity or an eclectic spirituality. They are happy to go with the flow and feel out of control and may become rebellious or demotivated if faced with a restrictive routine. They can be intrigued by the infinite progression of the mystical tradition. To grow in their prayer lives, perceiving pray-ers need to retain their sense of freedom but to overlay it with a form of discipline. Great riches may be found in the Anglican Daily Office, for example.

Outside comfort zone

With their Dominant Introverted Thinking function leading them to dislike muddled thought and unclear expression, INTPs are the most likely type to exercise their Christian ministry in an academic context so that they can be assured of having access to a constant stream of innovative high-quality ideas and then engaging in deep and meaningful intellectual intercourse. Pastoral care in a parish context is, therefore, unlikely to be an INTP's favourite way of spending time. Their cerebral bent, combined with their preference for Introversion, will make INTPs highly selective about their pastoral encounters and they will typically find the daily pastoral round draining.

Worship for INTPs will ideally be quiet and internally focused, visionary, with intellectual meat to chew on in a loose open-ended structure that allows for spontaneity. Leading worship will typically be draining (Introversion) and the constraints of a formal liturgy may well be irksome (Perceiving). The INTP Dominant function of Introverted Thinking will always seek to get to the bottom of an intellectual problem, to understand, and most worship experiences may well be too focused on the heart rather than the head.

Concern for the church fabric will not rate highly on the INTP's pleasure scale. The fine detail of wonky weathercocks or dysfunctional lightning conductors will pass the INTP by, and any hint of a regular maintenance schedule for church equipment will risk inducing terminal boredom. Similarly, the detailed minutiae involved in administration will drain the iNtuitive INTP and the need to plan ahead will be too constraining for the Perceiving INTP.

The conduct of preparatory meetings for baptisms, funerals and weddings will be efficient and will get the job done. There will tend to be a lack of natural warmth and a focus on the nuts and bolts of the services themselves rather than the emotional human issues that will be around. It is likely that the occasional offices will be done to the general satisfaction of the 'consumers' but the use of the less preferred Extraversion and Feeling functions will again be tiring.

INTPs are not great doers and tend not to be emotionally stirred by the needs of others, so it is unlikely that the intellectual concern INTPs will have for those among whom they minister will issue in social action.

The round of regular and ad hoc church meetings will typically be a trial for INTPs because they entail Extraverted interaction with others (Introversion) and adherence to a schedule (Perceiving), and often get enmeshed in trivia (Thinking). If there could be a guarantee that a meeting would tackle an intellectual conundrum, the INTP would be first in the queue to get started.

Stress response

If the INTP's working environment is one where he or she is under supervision and being required to work to strict rules and regulations, this will begin to be stressful. If that supervision is being done by somebody the INTP views as incompetent, the stress will increase. If work colleagues are similarly incompetent, and especially if the INTP is either responsible for or dependent on their work, this will only increase the feeling of stress. Illogicality, injustice or unfairness will all be stressors. If the working environment allows too little time for being alone, if the workspace is crowded or if the INTP is required to work in an Extraverted mode, especially with raw emotions in play, this will indicate that a stress response is not far off.

The first stage of a major stress response will be an exaggeration of the Dominant function. So for a Dominant Introverted Thinker there will be snap judgements expressed in caustic tones, and those judgements will have been based on little or no data. As INTPs journey further into their 'grip' response they will tend to become increasingly cutting and vicious. With little or no data being gathered, there will be increasing failure of conscious, rational Thinking until they 'flip' into their Inferior Extraverted Feeling function.

Once this flip has occurred the Introverted Thinker may become obsessive about using logic, overly sensitive to relationship issues, highly emotional and often loud and obnoxious. So INTPs in the grip of their Inferior Extraverted Feeling function will tend to become easily upset – whether or not they give expression to those emotions – and often forgetful and disorganized. They may feel profoundly alienated and become seriously concerned that they may have permanently lost control of their feelings and their emotions. They may express a passive-aggressive feeling of dissatisfaction, whining on in a petulant tone, and be highly sensitive to any sign that they are being ignored, disregarded or even disliked.

It is most unusual for INTPs to be able to reverse the flip directly and return to their Dominant function. For Dominant Introverted Thinkers in the grip of Inferior Extraverted Feeling, one way out will be the use – with help – of the Tertiary Sensing function: by getting hold of some facts and hard data that contradict the basis on which felt hurt has developed, it should be possible to begin to see things more in perspective and gradually re-establish their equilibrium. INTPs will need both physical and psychological space to make this adjustment, ideally being excused from some of their usual responsibilities – a conviction that they are unable to perform well will be common.

In the often lonely exercise of Christian ministry the INTP may need to seek such permission from a more senior colleague. It will be important that others do not ask how the INTP is feeling.

Life-giving strategies

INTPs will benefit from learning how and when to challenge others and not to get mired in minor nitpicking arguments. They would also do well to check that the assumptions they have made are firmly rooted in reality and also to develop their stickability, so that they can take tasks or projects to completion rather than just giving up either when they lose interest or when something more interesting turns up.

INTPs will also find that an understanding that their own emotions and feelings should not be ignored is important – expressing these can often help in avoiding the extremes of hypersensitivity and being overly self-critical when bottled-up emotions erupt. They would also do well to accept that the feelings of others are valid and not merely a sign of intellectual weakness. Taking time to think through what impact something they are about to say will have on the feelings of others will help INTPs to temper their usual forthright mode of expression.

INTPs are driven by their Introverted Thinking function to try and understand everything and then slot it into its rightful place in their internal model. They also continually acquire new information (Extraverted iNtuition) – nuances, impressions and intuitions – each piece of which generates new possibilities. These too have to be evaluated, understood and slotted into place. The Perceiving preference inclines INTPs to go on and on acquiring information, so the task of understanding and slotting-in is never fully completed because there is a constant flow of new information. INTPs will benefit from learning when to stop – not only their continual 'research' but also their leaping down yet another rabbit-hole. This may be helped by a conscious attempt to plan and set priorities and also by a determination to finish what has been started.

While they do need to nurture themselves with time alone for thinking, INTPs will benefit from understanding that other people need affirmation, appreciation and friendship and that social time spent with close friends is not time wasted.

Summary

INTPs are intellectually agile, analytical, detached, critical seekers after truth, and can be seen as being 'too clever by three-quarters'. With their tendency to ignore rules, hierarchy and bureaucracy, INTPs focus their energies on creative problem-solving, mostly in the abstract. They lead by the quality of their ideas, allow autonomy and encourage independent thinking with little or no bureaucratic noise. Life can be even richer for INTPs if they begin to appreciate that their own feelings, and those of others, are valid, and that close personal relationships can bring a unique joy.

15

Introducing the ENTP leader – the Enterprising Explorer

Dominant Extraverted iNtuition with Introverted Thinking

———◆·◆·◆———

ENTPs are energetic original thinkers who focus on the future. Witty and articulate, they are committed to discovering and exploring new possibilities, tend to be abstract and theoretical and can be brutally blunt when expounding their ideas and opinions over and against others.

* * *

Introduction

ENTPs are driven to understand the world they inhabit, working with concepts rather than facts to resolve complex problems, seeing possibilities in the present for future development, preferably working with other independent thinkers. Independent and analytical, ENTPs have a tendency to be dispassionate and objective but typically they are perceptive about other people's viewpoints and needs. Strongly entrepreneurial, ENTPs pick up ideas and possibilities like magpies and are outstanding at beginning projects but not so good at finishing them.

Type dynamics tell us that ENTPs have a Dominant Extraverted iNtuitive function, scanning the outer world for possibilities, new and exciting ideas and options many and varied. Their Auxiliary Introverted Thinking function applies objective reason and logic to the assessment of these new ideas and to planning how they might be realized. The Tertiary Extraverted Feeling function brings the needs and perspectives of other people into the equation, while the Inferior Introverted Sensing function allows the restrictions imposed by reality to be considered.

The four functions are used in four steps, one after the other – Dominant, Auxiliary, Tertiary and Inferior – but it is an unconscious, and very fast, process. The Tertiary and Inferior functions may be used minimally or not at all. If used, they may be less well executed, or even omitted altogether, if they have undergone little or no development. So in problem-solving, ENTPs will first grab as many ideas and possibilities as they can from thin air (Extraverted iNtuition) before subjecting them to a rigorous internal examination using logic and reason (Introverted Thinking). The impact that various possibilities might have on others is next considered (Extraverted Feeling), then the restrictions and constraints of practicality, including those from the ENTP's memory, will be allowed to have airtime (Introverted Sensing).

The top priority in the life of ENTPs is obtaining knowledge and passing it on. Theirs is a continual search for meaning in life and they tend to view everything as a task, including play-time. ENTPs place a high value on logic, coherence, knowledge and mastery of their subject, and have an overriding need to be competent. Rather than seeking power, they want to add continually to their intellectual armoury. ENTPs are among the pioneers of the type world, often making accurate predictions and being deeply satisfied by the process of problem-solving. If an ENTP were to come up with a prototype before anybody else, that would represent ENTP heaven – it does not get any better than being right *and* being first.

ENTPs value the intellectual process very highly – their Introverted Thinking preference compels them to pursue their quest for understanding, for getting to the bottom of whatever intellectual conundrum is to hand, indeed to eradicate error once and for all. They can be remarkably unconcerned about the sensitivities of others; it has been said that if one is not prepared to hear the unvarnished truth bluntly spoken, do not ask an iNtuitive Thinker for an opinion. One downside of this quest for the ultimate answer is that ENTPs can be seduced into delaying what might be very necessary immediate action by the appearance of another fascinating goal.

In a team environment ENTPs are compelling advocates of the causes they espouse, with their enthusiasm and visionary picture building. They are very gifted at melding the differing views of other members of the team into a cohesive whole but may upset their fellow team members by hogging the limelight. As well as bringing great energy and enterprise to the team, ENTPs can be quite competitive; but their attitude that nothing is impossible is contagious. Being somewhat butterfly minded, ENTPs can flit off to the next attractive intellectual puzzle without finishing what they have started.

ENTPs have little or no time for traditional ways of doing things that are revered merely because they *are* the traditional ways, so they can ignore a tried and trusted method simply because it has been tried before. This appetite for new things does help ENTPs to be among the first to recognize the value of any major change that might be proposed, and they are very gifted at developing and articulating creative new possibilities. There may be a danger of their taking on too many things at once or of giving up once things become everyday and hum-drum. ENTPs can be relied on to come up with a number of different perspectives when the team is faced with an issue, and their analytical questioning helps the team explore the virtues of the different possible solutions thoroughly.

As leaders ENTPs exemplify entrepreneurial aspiration and will challenge both themselves and those they lead to ever-greater heights – standards are always escalating. Although they are truly inspirational, ENTPs can be very forceful and push others beyond their limits. Valuing the quality of a person's thought over the person can be perceived as unaffirming, but ENTPs tend to be generous with their praise and affirmation when another's work is good. Always reaching for the stars, and refusing to believe that the impossible is unachievable, ENTPs continually strive for excellence and beyond. Unfettered by petty bureaucracy, ENTPs get the best out of those they lead by genuinely viewing themselves as *primus inter pares*, although some hectoring, cajoling and badgering may occur, to push people further than they thought they could go.

Comfort zone

ENTPs are happiest in the world of ideas, concepts, possibilities and opportunities. The development of a new parish vision, mission statement and strategic goals will be meat and drink to ENTPs. Developing and exploring lots of different possible directions, articulating the pros and cons of each and finding many and varied implementation possibilities will all be hugely energizing for them. The problem will be knowing when to stop.

Equally, the discovery of fresh gospel truths, wrestling with the hard questions of faith, challenging long-held religious traditions and finding new answers to old questions will enliven the ENTP's sermon preparation. Soaring visions of the future, radical approaches to the life of faith and knotty questions for the congregation to chew on will be the stuff of the ENTP sermon. ENTPs will much prefer to develop their own teaching course rather than use one developed by somebody else. Such a course will contain substantial amounts of intellectual meat and course sessions will be in danger of overrunning as new material strikes the ENTP in flight.

ENTPs will prefer spontaneous, open-ended visionary worship that is relational, vocal and intellectual. Leading worship, especially with large congregations, will tend to be energizing for ENTPs, and the opportunities for engaging with other minds will make post-worship coffee times congenial.

Prayer for ENTPs will primarily be an intellectual exercise. Bible study may well become prayer and there will be a constant search for truth and meaning. Church doctrine will be an important element in shaping the spirituality of ENTPs, and there may be some difficulty in bridging the gap between head and heart. Symbology will be intriguing to ENTPs – their fecund imaginations will take great joy in developing myriad things the symbols might represent. Mysticism may appeal to ENTPs but the drive to understand everything generated by the Auxiliary Introverted Thinking preference will probably need a more grounded approach.

Engaging with people in the external world will appeal to the ENTP's Extraversion preference but pastoral encounters will tend to be satisfying only if intellectual engagement is possible. Chance encounters are likely to be preferable to organized visits and new people in the parish will be most warmly welcomed if they bring some intellectual horsepower.

A parish setting that allows flexibility and variety and offers new and unexpected experiences will be exciting and energizing for ENTPs. Spontaneity and a lack of routine, with the freedom to be intellectually creative, will be an ideal environment for them.

Outside comfort zone

The routine and detail of parish administration and regular business meetings are likely to be draining for ENTPs, except when they present an intellectual challenge. The essentially solitary nature of the administrative process will not appeal to the Extravert ENTP and the concentration on facts and details of church fabric considerations will be equally unappealing.

Dealings with parishioners will be ruled by the head rather than the heart, so ENTPs will typically pursue fairness and justice over grace and mercy, and will approach decisions and pastoral problems with logic and reason.

The essentially touchy-feely nature of the occasional offices will be something of a trial for ENTPs, although great creativity may be applied to the preparation of candidates and the development of appropriate liturgies. Baptism parents may offer some intellectual diversion (even though their infants do not), as may wedding couples. However, ENTPs will typically find the irrationality and emotionalism of the grieving process at best bewildering and at worst incomprehensible.

Stimulated by the intellectual challenge and a host of possibilities, ENTPs may well come up with some superb ideas for social-action projects; but their implementation will best be left to others.

Stress response

ENTPs work best in an environment that recognizes and encourages their innovative problem-solving skills and their passion for all things new, and where the implementation of these great new ideas can be left to somebody else. Ideally ENTPs will not be trammelled by pettifogging rules and regulations or by having to conform to 'the way we do things round here'. They will work best surrounded by other intellects willing to innovate, preferably people who are expert in their own fields and can work independently. ENTPs need recognition for their creativity and originality and can work on a number of things simultaneously.

Because they welcome and embrace the future, ENTPs are at their best in fast-moving, rapidly changing environments.

Stimulated and challenged by seemingly intractable problems, they work best when left to their own devices, exploring new possibilities. Competitive and ambitious, ENTPs are fed by recognition and reward for what they achieve and are happiest in work environments that appreciate them for being resourceful in pursuing a variety of interests with little or no need of supervision. Flexible, varied, rapidly changing environments suit ENTPs down to the ground. Affable and sociable, they are happy to encourage others to join them in their enthusiastic pursuit of their goals.

Work will begin to become stressful when rules and regulations bring predictability and constraint and the achievement of assigned tasks is closely monitored and measured. Where work is not intellectually challenging, where supervisors are hidebound and closed to new ideas, where independence of thought and action is discouraged and where significant amounts of detail are required, this will cause ENTPs increasing levels of stress.

Stress levels will continue to increase if ENTPs are required to constrain their creative thinking or if their intellectual competence is called into question. Having to work with too many details under close supervision, especially if it is incompetent, will be a nightmare for ENTPs. Signs that the stress is getting to them often involve ENTPs taking on more and more work, becoming argumentative or passive aggressive, and becoming less and less effective.

A number of factors – fatigue and physical exhaustion, especially if caused by taking on too much, eating and sleeping too little – may cause ENTPs to trigger their Inferior function and result in the body reacting by developing a physical illness. Too much detailed work over an extended period can cause a similar reaction, especially if it entails battling the bureaucrats.

It is reasonably common for individuals to exaggerate their Dominant function just before they fall into the grip of their

Inferior function. For an ENTP this would probably look like the development of a plethora of ideas and possibilities, none of which had been subjected to the usual rigorous critical analysis. As this lopsidedness becomes less and less effective, the usual energy and enthusiasm ENTPs have for their work deteriorates into gloom and despondency.

The ENTP's 'flip' into the Inferior function of Introverted Sensing often presents as an obsessive concentration on irrelevant details, with all big-picture perspective lost. This focus on internal processing is unnatural and uncomfortable for ENTPs, so energy drains away and they can become withdrawn and depressed, convinced they are not and never have been lovable. This may lead to an unhealthy focus on the state of their own physical health, and ENTPs can become acutely aware of their own bodies and may imagine that they are developing all sorts of physical symptoms. Obsessive surfing of medical advice sites on the Internet can feed this tendency to hypochondria, and only the direst of possible explanations will be deemed correct.

If one likens life to a game of Snakes and Ladders, the experience of descending into the grip of the Inferior function can feel like landing on the head of the longest snake and ending up virtually back at the start. As with the board game, it is highly unusual to land immediately on the bottom rung of the ladder that takes you back to where you came from. A solution that often works is to take the smallest ladder available, represented by the Tertiary function; ENTPs have a Tertiary function of Feeling. It is highly unlikely that one can make this journey by one's own efforts, so ENTPs need a trusted friend or colleague, adept at using their own Feeling function, to help in the process of recovery.

ENTPs can be helped to become aware that their current actions are likely to be violating their own internal value system, and that what they are doing to themselves disrupts the harmony of their family and work groups. Once that is recognized, ENTPs can be encouraged to take sufficient rest, to respond to their bodily needs in a gentle, restorative way, perhaps coupled with some mild physical exercise. Refusing to take on any more tasks and rigorously prioritizing and/or delegating current tasks can begin to relieve some of the pressure. With returning physical health and a lessening of the pressures of task completion, ENTPs can bring the analytical perspective of their Auxiliary Introverted Thinking to bear, shining the light of logic and reason on the irrational state in which they have been. Once that has been accomplished, normal service can be resumed.

Life-giving strategies

ENTPs get stressed when having to work under time pressure, so developing some time-management skills would bear fruit. Prioritizing tasks and really accepting that time is not infinite can help relieve the pressure. Also, developing the self-discipline to complete one task before leaping off into another would pay dividends.

ENTPs would do well to build some regular physical exercise into their daily routine, to be gentle with themselves and to learn to listen to their bodies. It is hoped that ENTPs who are in Christian ministry will have a regular prayer discipline, but this may benefit from being further developed along more meditational lines.

Developing their skills of active listening would help ENTPs to become more aware of other people's feelings, and moderating their tendency to be blunt and uncompromising in their opinions and feedback would help them be less abrasive in their dealings with others. Equally, a more developed awareness of their own feelings – and an increasing facility in expressing them – would be good.

Compromise will always be uncongenial to ENTPs but finding ways of conceding gracefully would be of benefit, as would occasionally asking for help. This should not be seen as a sign of weakness or incompetence but as a recognition that no one can be good at everything.

Summary

ENTPs are continually in search of new opportunities and possibilities, spotting patterns and interconnectivity that escape others, often seeming to others to be almost prescient. Having developed a number of conceptual futures, they are adept at bringing to bear their logical reason to critique them within a strategic framework. Instinctively understanding organizational systems, ENTPs are past masters at making the system work for them. Innovative and creative, ENTPs are funny, articulate and powerful but have no illusions about themselves. They love an argument and love having the last word. ENTPs will benefit from learning to listen more, and more attentively, and from developing some stickability – finishing what they have started. They would also do well to get more in touch not only with their own feelings but also the feelings of others, and to develop an internal monitor that assesses the impact of a remark or opinion before it is articulated. Life will also be more serene if ENTPs can *really* accept that total omnicompetence is unachievable.

16

Introducing the ENTJ leader – the Decisive Strategist

Dominant Extraverted Thinking with Introverted iNtuition

———•◦•———

ENTJs are quick-witted, original, innovative problem-solvers with a natural flair for leadership. Intelligent and percep-tive, they are quick, assertive and positive, making decisions with clarity and logic, and seldom troubled by second thoughts.

* * *

Introduction

ENTJs are natural leaders who are always striving to find a better way, relishing problems and developing original and innovative solutions. Always wanting to understand, predict, explain, they seek out challenges and maintain a lively interest in all things. Intellectually voracious, ENTJs can usually be relied on to hold well-thought-out views on almost anything. Disliking routine, illogicality and woolliness of thought, they can be perceived as dismayingly competent, uncomfortably intimidating and as having ridiculously high standards.

Type dynamics tell us that ENTJs have a Dominant function of Extraverted Thinking that helps them to direct people and resources decisively and structure their environment to achieve their long-term goals. The Auxiliary function of Introverted iNtuition helps ENTJs develop strategies, patterns and possibilities for both the present and the future. The Tertiary Extraverted Sensing function makes them aware of the detailed steps and stages that will be needed to achieve their goals. The Inferior function of Introverted Feeling filters ENTJs' developing world view through the mesh of the their internal value system.

The four functions are used in four steps, one after the other – Dominant, Auxiliary, Tertiary and Inferior – but it is an unconscious, and very fast, process. The Tertiary and Inferior functions may be used minimally or not at all. If used, they may be less well executed, or even omitted altogether, if they have undergone little or no development. When approaching a problem, then, the first lens used by ENTJs will be that of reason and logic, assembling the human, financial and other resources that may be needed on initial analysis of the issue at hand (Extraverted Thinking). Then a wide range of possible solutions will be rapidly developed (Introverted iNtuition), each being subjected to the analytical process. Facts and figures, details and data will then be gathered to fine-tune the solutions being developed (Sensing), before the potential impact on people and their values and feelings, and the ENTJ's own internal value system, are brought into the equation (Introverted Feeling).

The top priority in the life of an ENTJ is obtaining knowledge and passing it on. Theirs is a continual search for meaning in life and ENTJs tend to view everything as a task, including playtime. They place a high value on logic, coherence, knowledge and mastery of their subject, and have an overriding need to be competent. Rather than seeking power, ENTJs want to add continually to their intellectual armoury. They are among the pioneers of the type world, often making accurate predictions and being deeply satisfied by the process of problem-solving. If an ENTJ were to come up with a prototype before anybody else, that would represent ENTJ heaven.

ENTJs value the intellectual process very highly – their Extraverted Thinking preference compels them to pursue their quest for understanding a situation thoroughly so that the solution can be developed and implemented and the job can get done. One downside of this quest for the ultimate answer is that ENTJs can be seduced into delaying what might be very necessary immediate action by the appearance of another fascinating goal.

ENTJs can be remarkably unconcerned about the sensitivities of others; it has been said that if one is not prepared to hear the unvarnished truth bluntly spoken, do not ask an intuitive thinker for an opinion. ENTJs are sometimes kept on the margins or at a distance because they can present as very intimidating.

As leaders ENTJs can be tough-minded, setting very high standards, and are happy to take the lead quickly and decisively. As with the other iNtuitive Thinkers, incompetence is anathema to ENTJs, especially in themselves; and they are not ones to suffer fools gladly, if at all. They can present as impatient, insensitive and uncaring, and even downright arrogant.

Comfort zone

With their Dominant Extraverted Thinking function combining with their Auxiliary Introverted iNtuition function, ENTJs are instinctive problem-solvers who relish tackling challenges and the complexities they bring, in order to come up with innovative solutions. Wrestling with the hard problems of faith and, ideally, coming up with new ways of looking at them will energize and deeply satisfy ENTJs.

They enjoy raising faith issues that others find difficulty answering and will find preaching and teaching very satisfying. Sermons will tend to be logically constructed progressions from known to unknown, raising and answering tough issues, often leaving the congregation with some work to do on the intriguing questions with which they are left at the end of the sermon.

The Extraversion preference of the ENTJ means that energy will be drawn from the relational and vocal aspects of worship – ENTJs are likely to be fizzing after a morning of leading worship, with their Thinking function relishing the opportunity for intellectual interaction with members of the congregation following the services. The worship style will preferably be structured and controlled (Judging), with lots of intellectual meat (Thinking) and a sense of the awe and wonder of what could be possible (iNtuition).

The Thinking preference, combined with the visionary orientation of the iNtuitive, will make the ENTJ comfortable with creating a challenging framework for the future of the parish, sector or area of responsibility; visionary thinking and setting strategic goals will be almost second nature to ENTJs. Because they will always be seeking to improve themselves, ENTJs will be keen to develop others, especially if they are responsible for training more junior clergy. While this may take the form of coaching, ENTJs will be more comfortable with mentoring – the non-directive approach of the coach will be difficult for an ENTJ to maintain. The ENTJ's Thinking function will occasionally lead to somewhat insensitive handling of performance that is less than excellent – indeed, ENTJs may be experienced as unreasonably critical and demanding. It has to be said, however, that ENTJs demand no less of themselves.

For the Extraverted pray-er, God is revealed in the outer world of people, things and activities. While ENTJs may find too much silence daunting, they may enjoy some time in silence, but spending time on inner-world processes will tend to be tiring. The Thinking pray-er will like structure and dislike repetition. Intelligibility will be important, as will the exercise of logic and reason. The search for truth and meaning will be a continual one, and God tends to be found in the mind and in experience. The doctrine of the church to which the thinker belongs will be important. Bible study will actually become prayer in the classical sense of reading and meditating on the word. Emotionalism in worship or prayer, or numinous religious experiences, will be thought suspect. The iNtuition function will respond to symbols that can represent numinous mystery and intriguing possibilities but this will usually be in the context of the orderly prayer preferred by the judging pray-er – well-organized prayer and worship times, with a logical structure. Familiarity will be preferred over novelty, and the use of set liturgical forms of prayer will be comforting. Order, structure and discipline will be very important, not only as the form that carries them through times of barrenness but also as a stable base on which a more open style can be built.

Because they will typically gain energy from being with people and exercising their intellectual muscles, chairing meetings such as the parochial church council or the annual parochial church meeting will be comfortable for the ENTJ. The Judging orientation will be at home with the order and structure of the agenda, the Thinking function will be able to meet and handle issues objectively and rationally as they arise during the meeting and the iNtuiting function will be able to hear the music as well as the words in the interplay between those attending the meeting. This will allow opportunities for enabling and facilitating the contributions of the more reticent and the avoidance of too many excursions into territory more properly the concern of another forum – particularly where there is a tendency to repeat work already done at an inappropriate level of detail.

The ENTJ's Judging preference will need plans and schedules for comfort. Worship services should start on time and should follow the planned structure (although the iNtuitive preference may have planned-in something just a little different this week). ENTJs will often need the reassurance of a to-do list – sometimes writing down tasks that have already been completed that day, just so they can be crossed off. What a sense of achievement that brings.

The routine and detail of parish administration and regular business meetings are likely to appeal to the Judging function of ENTJs, especially when they present an intellectual challenge, as they enjoy organizing, planning and leading. The essentially solitary nature of the administrative process will not appeal to the Extravert ENTJ. When it comes to church fabric, while ENTJs can be excited by the possibilities that a re-ordering might bring, concentration on the essentially sensory nature of the facts and details of church fabric considerations will be unappealing.

Outside comfort zone

Dealings with parishioners will be ruled by the head rather than the heart, so ENTJs will typically pursue fairness and justice over grace and mercy, and will approach decisions and pastoral problems with logic and reason. Emotional encounters with parishioners will be uncomfortable and dealing with their emotional issues will not come easily to ENTJs. Their responses will tend to be very rational and potentially insensitive to the emotional needs of those they are with.

The essentially touchy-feely nature of the occasional offices will be something of a trial for ENTJs, although great creativity may be applied to the preparation of candidates and the development of appropriate liturgies. Baptism parents may offer some intellectual diversion (even though their infants do not), as may wedding couples. However, ENTJs will typically find the irrationality and emotionalism of the grieving process at best bewildering and at worst incomprehensible.

Stimulated by the intellectual challenge and a host of possibilities, ENTJs may well come up with some excellent ideas for social-action projects and will be superb at leading them; but the detailed implementation will best be left to others.

Stress response

ENTJs thrive in work environments that require them to take charge and bring their independent judgement to bear. They are committed to right order and will want to develop, and then work within, well-defined organizational structures where the most important thing is to meet targets and achieve goals. Work itself is typically affirming for ENTJs but they do like to have clarity about structures, roles and responsibilities. They like to work on practical, realistic, concrete tasks with well-defined deliverables that are tangible. ENTJs like predictability within an environment that allows them to work at their own pace.

If ENTJs begin to lose control over their own time and the tasks they are engaged in, work can start to become stressful. Lack of order, blurred roles and responsibilities and disorganization will cause ENTJs to perform less well than they would normally expect to, and their consequent increasing incompetence will add to the stress. If this is combined with a fluid environment where the smooth task flow is often interrupted, or where ENTJs are required to work in a way that seems illogical, the stress levels will continue to increase.

The Auxiliary function of ENTJs is Introverted Feeling. A major characteristic of Introverted Feelers is the need for life to be in harmony with their own internal value system. This deep, intense code will often lead Introverted Feelers to espouse one or more causes and to offer, and demand, intense loyalty. If and when something is at odds with this value system, it absolutely has to be put right. ENTJs are not good at showing how they feel and will certainly not advertise any passion they may feel about a cause they value highly. It will be very stressful for ENTJs if one of these core values is somehow violated – for example, if an ENTJ is passionately anti-vivisection and someone is being actively critical of a relevant demonstration or flippant about animal research, this will be perceived as extremely stressful and may trigger a 'grip' response.

ENTJs are not good at being demonstrative or at dealing with others who are quick to show their emotions. If ENTJs find themselves in a work environment where emotions run high, they will feel really uncomfortable and tend to exaggerate their rationality and objectivity. ENTJs tend to be somewhat blunt and insensitive in pointing out flaws or in taking the hard decisions that may have a significant negative impact on others. If their stress levels are already high, ENTJs may be plagued with memories of past decisions, comments or actions that have hurt others and become harshly self-critical. This too can trigger a grip response.

It is not unusual for individuals to overemphasize their Dominant function just before falling off the cliff into the grip of their Inferior function. ENTJs may become more and more detached and unemotional, act as coldly rational and dictatorial and make blunt pronouncements about snap decisions that have little or no data to support them. Rigidity of attitude and a withdrawal from emotional engagement with anybody may occur.

Once the Inferior function of Introverted Feeling has been triggered, ENTJs tend to become highly tuned to their own internal emotional responses and to those of others. Inoffensive remarks can be perceived as deeply wounding; any indication that they are not being valued will be taken as evidence of exclusion or rejection and there may be some form of persecution complex. As they are so unused to using their Feeling function and expressing their emotions, when their feelings run high, ENTJs tend to overdo it – outbursts of fury, overbearing behaviour, cutting remarks. However, because ENTJs have such a high need to be in control, they may work extremely hard to disguise the fact that their emotions are running high, often saving their outbursts for the safety of home. Often ENTJs will be frightened or perplexed by these emotions surging through them and may feel that there is something wrong with them. This can lead to anxiety and depression.

As ever with a grip experience, it is highly unlikely that individuals can get themselves out of the grip by their own efforts. A trusted friend, preferably an iNtuitive Sensor, to whom an ENTJ can unburden him- or herself, who will gently listen and not judge or intrude, will be a good first step. The ladder of functions that needs to be climbed in order for an ENTJ to regain equilibrium should start with the Tertiary Sensing function – hence the value of the iNtuitive Sensor as the friend in need. If the ENTJ can be helped to access his or her Tertiary Sensing function – finding some hard evidence that all is not lost, that the picture is not all black, spending some time alone, undertaking some gentle physical activity, indulging in an appreciation of the beauty of nature – this can help to take the first steps on the journey back. Once the Sensing function has been re-engaged, it may be possible to help ENTJs use their Auxiliary iNtuition to see their current state in a wider context – even to see that their current behaviour actually violates their internal value system – and that a brighter future can lie ahead. That done, the ENTJ can finally return to equilibrium with his or her Dominant Thinking function restored.

Life-giving strategies

It is reasonably common for ENTJs to have a very short grip experience because they have an innate ability to treat such episodes as yet another task to be tackled, and so develop strategies for themselves that minimize the impact of the experience.

It would benefit ENTJs to allow their feelings some expression in a controlled way – perhaps exploring their feelings for, and even with, those who are nearest and dearest or going with the emotional surge of a great symphony or love story. Trying to consider the impact of an explosive outburst before indulging in it would be of benefit. This might also help ENTJs be more gentle with people – both in a work context and in social intercourse. Working on their active listening skills would also help ENTJs in this endeavour, as would learning to praise more and criticize less, especially those who are inexperienced.

Relinquishing some measure of control, sometimes even allowing life to pass by unplanned and being happy to be surprised by the unexpected, would help ENTJs be less uptight. Playing with their Sensing function by trying out some creative pursuits, either actively or passively (painting, working with clay, art appreciation), might act as a mild release if tension is building. Taking some time for reflection before leaping into action might also help ENTJs be more balanced.

Summary

ENTJs are natural leaders and organizers. Intelligent, articulate and confident, they bring energy and originality to the task of problem-solving. With their highly developed presence and personal power, ENTJs are charismatic magnets who draw others to their cause. They decide quickly and communicate easily and are always on the lookout for improvement in themselves, those they lead and the organizations to which they belong. With a tendency to be outspoken and critical, ENTJs would benefit from being less hard on themselves and on those they serve.

Taking it further

If this has sparked some interest and you would like to take it further, it is likely that the regional or national centre for your church will know of qualified practitioners who can help. There are a number of key areas in which psychological type can help, including

- problem-solving and conflict
- teamworking
- leadership
- communication
- change
- stress management.

As a registered Myers-Briggs® practitioner, I consult to individuals, church staff teams and church councils, and have run workshops on type and prayer and spirituality, as well as using type in my spiritual direction practice.

Other avenues include the British Association of Psychological Type (BAPT), which holds a register of practitioners at <www.bapt.org.uk/type-practitioners>. OPP (formerly Oxford Psychologists Press) holds the copyright for the MBTI® in the United Kingdom and they offer a variety of training and consultancy resources; see <www.opp.com/en>. Assessment, consultancy and coaching services are also offered by the Type Academy (<http://type-academy.co.uk>) and Team Focus Ltd (<http://teamfocus.co.uk/index.php>).

Notes

Foreword

1 On the use of this spelling in the present volume, see note 7 of 'Psychological type theory' below.

Introduction

1 Lee, C. and Horsman, S. (2002), *Affirmation and Accountability: The Society of Mary and Martha's Manual of Practical Suggestions for Preventing Clergy Stress, Sickness and Ill-Health Retirement*, Exeter: The Society of Mary and Martha, p. 29.

Psychological type theory

1 Allport, G. (1961), *Pattern and Growth in Personality*, New York: Holt, Rinehart & Winston, p. 28.

2 Weinberg, R. S. and Gould, D. (2011), *Foundations of Sport and Exercise Psychology*, Leeds: Human Kinetics, p. 47.

3 From <www.apa.org/topics/personality>.

4 Francis, L. J. (2005), *Faith and Psychology: Personality, Religion and the Individual*, London: Darton, Longman & Todd, p. 7.

5 Montgomery, S. (2002), *People Patterns: A Modern Guide to the Four Temperaments*, Del Mar, CA: Archer.

6 Galton, Francis (1884), 'Measurement of Character', *Fortnightly Review* 36, pp. 179–85.

7 Common usage spells 'extroversion' with an 'o'. In his introduction to the general description of the types, Jung states: 'In the following pages I shall attempt a general description of the psychology of the types, starting with the two basic types I have termed introverted and extraverted', and he goes on to define these terms quite specifically. This book therefore uses the 'extra' spelling where appropriate – Jung, C. G. (1992), *Psychological Types*, Oxford: Routledge, p. 330.

8 Briggs Myers, I., rev. L. K. Kirby and K. D. Myers (2000), *Introduction to Type: A Guide to Understanding Your Results on the Myers-Briggs Type Indicator*, Oxford: OPP.

9 Keirsey, D. and Bates, M. (1984), *Please Understand Me: Character and Temperament Types*, Del Mar, CA: Prometheus Nemesis; Keirsey, D. (1998), *Please Understand Me II: Temperament, Character, Intelligence*, Del Mar, CA: Prometheus Nemesis.

10 Spranger, E. (1928), *Types of Men: The Psychology and Ethics of Personality*, trans. P. J. W. Pigors, Halle: Max Niemeyer.

11 Eysenck, H. J. and Eysenck, M. W. (1985), *Personality and Individual Differences: A Natural Science Approach*, New York: Plenum Press.

12 Costa, P. T. and McCrae, R. R. (1985), *The NEO Personality Inventory Manual*, Odessa, FL: Psychological Assessment Resources.

13 Cattell, R. B., Eber, H. W. and Tatsuoka, M. M. (1970), *Handbook for the Sixteen Personality Factor Questionnaire (16PF)*, Champaign, IL: Institute for Personality and Ability Testing.

14 Jung, C. G. (1992), *Psychological Types*, Oxford: Routledge.

15 Eysenck, H. J., Barrett, P., Wilson, G. and Jackson, C. (1992), 'Primary Trait Measurement of the 21 Components of the P-E-N System', *European Journal of Psychological Assessment* 8(2), pp. 109–17.

16 Digman, J. M. (1990), 'Personality Structure: Emergence of the Five-Factor Model', *Annual Review of Psychology* 41, pp. 417–40.

17 McCrae, R. R. and Costa, P. T. (1987), 'Validation of the Five-Factor Model of Personality Across Instruments and Observers', *Journal of Personality and Social Psychology* 52(1), pp. 81–90.

18 University of Kentucky, <www.uky.edu/Classes/PSY/313-001/traitapproachespart2.ppt>.

19 Nettle, D. (2007), *Personality: What Makes You The Way You Are*, Oxford: Oxford University Press.

20 <www.citehr.com/189400-16pf-questionnaire-primary-factors-definitions.html>.

Assessing psychological type

1 Lawrence, G. D. (2009), *People Types and Tiger Stripes: Using Psychological Type to Help Students Discover their Unique Potential*,

4th edn, Gainesville, FL: Center for Applications of Psychological Type, p. 18.

2 Bayne, R. (1995), *The Myers-Briggs Type Indicator®: A Critical Review and a Practical Guide*, London: Chapman & Hall.

3 Bayne, *Myers-Briggs Type Indicator®*, p. 88.

4 Bayne, *Myers-Briggs Type Indicator®*, p. 89.

5 Lloyd, J. B. (2012), 'The Myers-Briggs Type Indicator® and Mainstream Psychology: Analysis and Evaluation of an Unresolved Hostility', *Journal of Beliefs and Values* 33(1), pp. 23–4.

6 Lloyd, 'The Myers-Briggs Type Indicator® and Mainstream Psychology'.

7 Lloyd, 'The Myers-Briggs Type Indicator® and Mainstream Psychology'.

8 Francis, L. J. (2005), *Faith and Psychology: Personality, Religion and the Individual*, London: Darton, Longman & Todd.

9 Leech, K. (ed.) (1996), *Myers-Briggs: Some Critical Reflections*, Manchester: Blackfriars Publications.

10 Jung, C. G. (1992), *Psychological Types*, Oxford: Routledge, pp. 448–50.

11 Francis, *Faith and Psychology*, p. 94.

12 Francis, *Faith and Psychology*, p. 95.

13 <www.opp.com/en/Knowledge-centre/Blog/2016/January/How-should-we-respond-to-criticim-of-the-MBTI-assessment>.

14 Keirsey, D. and Bates, M. (1984), *Please Understand Me: Character and Temperament Types*, Del Mar, CA: Prometheus Nemesis.

15 Keirsey, D. (1998), *Please Understand Me II: Temperament, Character, Intelligence*, Del Mar, CA: Prometheus Nemesis.

16 Keirsey and Bates, *Please Understand Me*, p. 26.

17 Keirsey, *Please Understand Me II*, p. 18.

18 Francis, L. J., Craig, C. L. and Robbins, M. (2008), 'The Relationship Between the Keirsey Temperament Sorter and the Short-Form Revised Eysenck Personality Questionnaire', *Journal of Individual Differences* 29(2), pp. 116–20.

19 Briggs Myers, I., rev. L. K. Kirby and K. D. Myers (2000), *Introduction to Type: A Guide to Understanding Your Results on the Myers-Briggs Type Indicator*, Oxford: OPP, p. 34.

20 Kendall, E., Carr, S., Moyle, P. and Harris, L. (2006), *Myers-Briggs Type Indicator® User's Guide*, Oxford: OPP; Chadha, N. K. (2009), *Applied Psychometry*, London: Sage.

21 Chadha, *Applied Psychometry*, p. 259.

22 Francis, L. J. (2009), 'Psychological Type Theory and Religious and Spiritual Experiences', in M. de Souza, L. J. Francis, J. O'Higgins-Norman and D. G. Scott (eds), *International Handbook of Education for Spirituality, Care and Wellbeing*, Dordrecht, Heidelberg, London and New York: Springer, p. 130.

23 Francis, L. and Jones, S. H. (1999), 'The Scale Properties of the MBTI Form G (Anglicised) Among Adult Churchgoers', *Pastoral Sciences Journal* 18(1), pp. 107–26.

24 Francis, L. J., Craig, C. L. and Robbins, M. (2007), 'Two Different Operationalisations of Psychological Type: Comparing the Myers-Briggs Type Indicator and the Keirsey Temperament Sorter', in R. A. Degregorio (ed.), *New Developments in Psychological Testing*, New York: Nova Science, pp. 119–38, p. 130.

25 Francis et al., 'Two Different Operationalisations of Psychological Type', p. 68.

26 Francis, 'Psychological Type Theory', p. 131.

27 Fawcett, B. G., Francis, L. J. and Robbins, M. (2010), 'The Scale Properties of the Adolescent Form of the Francis Psychological Type Scales (FPTSA) Among Canadian Baptist Youth', *Pastoral Psychology* 60(2), pp. 201–16, p. 205.

Discovering the type profile of Christian leaders

1 See <www.st-marys-centre.org.uk/courses/typeandfaith.html>.

2 Francis, L. J., Payne, V. J. and Jones, S. H. (2001), 'Psychological Types of Male Anglican Clergy in Wales', *Journal of Psychological Type* 56, pp. 19–23.

3 Francis, L. J. and Robbins, M. (2002), 'Psychological Types of Male Evangelical Church Leaders', *Journal of Beliefs and Values* 23(2), pp. 217–20.

4 Francis, L. and Payne, J. V. (2002), 'The Payne Index of Ministry Styles (PIMS): Ministry Styles and Psychological Type Among

Male Anglican Clergy in Wales', *Research in the Social Scientific Study of Religion* 13, pp. 125–41.

5 Francis and Payne, 'The Payne Index of Ministry Styles', p. 139.

6 Craig, C. L., Horsfall, T. and Francis, L. J. (2005), 'Psychological Types of Male Missionary Personnel Training in England: A Role for Thinking Type Men?', *Pastoral Psychology* 53(5), pp. 475–82.

7 Craig, Horsfall and Francis, 'Psychological Types of Male Missionary Personnel', p. 478.

8 Craig, Horsfall and Francis, 'Psychological Types of Male Missionary Personnel', p. 481.

9 Francis, L. J., Craig, C. L., Horsfall, T. and Ross, C. F. J. (2005), 'Psychological Types of Male and Female Lay Church Leaders in England, Compared with United Kingdom Population Norms', *Fieldwork in Religion* 1(1), pp. 69–83.

10 Francis, L. J., Craig, C. L., Whinney, M., Tilley D. and Slater, P. (2007), 'Psychological Typology of Anglican Clergy in England: Diversity, Strengths, and Weaknesses in Ministry', *International Journal of Practical Theology* 11(2), pp. 266–84.

11 Francis, L. J., Craig, C. L. and Butler, A. (2007), 'Psychological Types of Male Evangelical Anglican Seminarians in England', *Journal of Psychological Type* 67, pp. 11–17.

12 Oswald, R. M. and Kroeger, O. (1988), *Personality Type and Religious Leadership*, Washington, DC: Alban Institute.

13 Kay, W. K. and Francis, L. J. (2008), 'Psychological Type Preferences of Female Bible College students in England', *Journal of Beliefs and Values* 29(1), pp. 101–5.

14 Francis, L. J., Robbins, M., Duncan, B. and Whinney, M. (2010), 'Confirming the Psychological Type Profile of Anglican Clergymen in England: A Ministry for Intuitives', in B. Ruelas and V. Briseno (eds), *Psychology of Intuition*, New York: Nova Science, pp. 211–19.

15 Francis, L. J. and Village, A. (2008), *Preaching With All Our Souls: A Study in Hermeneutics and Psychological Type*, London: Continuum, pp. 111–12.

16 Francis, L. J., Gubb, S. and Robbins, M. (2009), 'Psychological Type Profile of Lead Elders Within the Newfrontiers Network of Churches', *Journal of Beliefs and Values* 30(1), pp. 61–9.

17 Francis, Gubb and Robbins, 'Psychological Type Profile of Lead Elders', p. 67.

18 Francis et al., 'Confirming the Psychological Type Profile of Anglican Clergymen'.

19 Francis et al., 'Confirming the Psychological Type Profile of Anglican Clergymen', p. 217.

20 Francis, L. J., Whinney, M., Burton, L. and Robbins, M. (2011), 'Psychological Type Preferences of Male and Female Free Church Ministers in England', *Research in the Social Scientific Study of Religion* 22, pp. 251–63.

21 Francis et al., 'Psychological Type Preferences', p. 254.

22 Francis et al., 'Psychological Type Preferences', p. 254.

23 Francis, L. J., Robbins, M. and Whinney, M. (2011), 'Women Priests in the Church of England: Psychological Type Profile', *Religions* 2(3), pp. 389–97.

24 Kendall, E. (1998), *MBTI® European English Edition: Step I Manual Supplement*, Oxford: OPP.

25 Francis, Robbins and Whinney, 'Women Priests in the Church of England', p. 396.

26 Francis, L. J., Whinney, M. and Robbins, M. (2013), 'Who is Called to be a Bishop? A Study in Psychological Type Profiling of Bishops in the Church of England', *Journal of Beliefs and Values* 34(2), pp. 135–51.

27 Church of England (1662), *The Book of Common Prayer*, London: Everyman's Library, 1999.

28 Francis et al., 'Who is Called to be a Bishop?'

29 The Archbishops' Council (2000), *Common Worship*, London: Church House Publishing.

30 Francis et al., 'Who is Called to be a Bishop?', p. 16.

31 Francis et al., 'Who is Called to be a Bishop?', p. 17.

32 Francis et al., 'Who is Called to be a Bishop?', p. 18.

33 Francis et al., 'Psychological Types of Male and Female Lay Church Leaders'.

34 Francis, Gubb and Robbins, 'Psychological Type Profile of Lead Elders', p. 62.

35 Francis et al., 'Psychological Typology of Anglican Clergy'.

36 Francis et al., 'Confirming the Psychological Type Profile of Anglican Clergymen'.
37 Francis and Payne, 'The Payne Index of Ministry Styles'.

Discerning the influence of type on Christian leaders

1 Blizzard, S. W. (1955), 'The Roles of the Rural Parish Minister, the Protestant Seminaries, and the Science of Social Behavior', *Religious Education* 50(6), pp. 383–92; Blizzard, S. W. (1956), 'The Minister's Dilemma', *The Christian Century* 73, pp. 505–9; Blizzard, S. W. (1958), 'The Parish Minister's Self-Image of His Master Role', *Pastoral Psychology* 9(9), pp. 25–32; Blizzard, S. W. (1958), 'The Protestant Parish Minister's Integrating Roles', *Religious Education* 53(4), pp. 374–80.

2 Nelsen, H. M., Yokley, R. L. and Madron, T. W. (1973), 'Ministerial Roles and Social Actionist Stance: Protestant Clergy and Protest in the Sixties', *American Sociological Review* 38(3), pp. 375–86.

3 Reilly, M. E. (1975), 'Perceptions of the Priest Role', *Sociological Analysis* 36(4), pp. 347–56.

4 Tiller, J. (1983), *A Strategy for the Church's Ministry*, London: Church Information Office.

5 Lauer, R. H. (1973), 'Organizational Punishment: Punitive Relations in a Voluntary Association: A Minister in a Protestant Church', *Human Relations* 26(2), pp. 189–202.

6 Francis, L. and Rodger, R. (1994), 'The Influence of Personality on Clergy Role Prioritization, Role Influences, Conflict and Dissatisfaction with Ministry', *Personality and Individual Differences* 16(6), pp. 947–57.

7 Robbins, M. and Francis, L. (2000), 'Role Prioritization among Clergywomen: The Influence of Personality and Church Tradition among Female Stipendiary Anglican Clerics in the UK', *British Journal of Theological Education* 11(1), pp. 7–23.

8 Davies, D., Watkins, C. and Winter, M. (1991), *Church and Religion in Rural England*, Edinburgh: T. & T. Clark.

9 Ranson, S., Bryman, A. and Hinings, B. (1977), *Clergy, Ministers and Priests*, London: Routledge & Kegan Paul.

10 Payne, J. V. (2001), 'Personality Type and Ministry: A Study of Personality Type and Clergy Satisfaction with Ministry', unpublished MPhil dissertation, University of Wales, Trinity College, Carmarthen.

11 Francis, L. and Payne, J. V. (2002), 'The Payne Index of Ministry Styles (PIMS): Ministry Styles and Psychological Type Among Male Anglican Clergy in Wales', *Research in the Social Scientific Study of Religion* 13, pp. 125–41.

12 Briggs Myers, I. with Myers, P. B. (1995), *Gifts Differing: Understanding Personality Type*, Mountain View, CA: Davies-Black; Briggs Myers, I., rev. Kirby, L. K. and Myers, K. D. (2000), *Introduction to Type: A Guide to Understanding Your Results on the Myers-Briggs Type Indicator*, Oxford: OPP.

13 Rogers, J. (2007), *Sixteen Personality Types: At Work In Organisations*, London: Management Futures.

14 Goldsmith, M. and Wharton, M. (1993), *Knowing Me, Knowing You: Exploring Personality Type and Temperament*, London: SPCK.

15 Spoto, A. (1995), *Jung's Typology in Perspective*, Boston, MA: Sigo Press.

16 Kroeger, O. and Thuesen, J. M. (1988), *TypeTalk: The 16 Personality Types That Determine How We Live, Love, and Work*, New York: Dell.

17 Kummerow, J. M., Barger, N. J. and Kirby, L. K. (1997), *Work Types: Understand Your Work Personality*, New York: Hachette.

18 Pearman, R. R. and Albritton, S. C. (1997), *I'm Not Crazy, I'm Just Not You: The Real Meaning of the 16 Personality Types*, Mountain View, CA: Davies-Black.

19 Bayne, R. (2004), *Psychological Types at Work: An MBTI Perspective*, London: Thomson Learning.

20 Barr, L. and Barr, N. (1993), *The Leadership Equation: Leadership, Management and the Myers-Briggs*, Austin, TX: Eakin Press.

21 Rogers, J. (2007), *Influencing Others Using the Sixteen Personality Types*, London: Management Futures.

22 Francis, L. (2008), 'Psychological Type and Leadership Styles: How to Discern Which Type of Leader You Are', in J. Nelson (ed.), *How to Become a Creative Church Leader*, Norwich: Canterbury Press, pp. 26–35.

23 Hirsh, E., Hirsh, K. W. and Krebs Hirsh, S. (2003), *Introduction to Type and Teams*, 2nd edn, Mountain View, CA: Consulting Psychologists Press.

24 Kendall, E., Carr, S., Moyle, P. and Harris, L. (2006), *Myers-Briggs Type Indicator® User's Guide*, Oxford: OPP, p. 37.

25 Thompson, H. L. (1996), *Jung's Function-Attitudes Explained*, Watkinsville, GA: Wormhole.

26 Myers, K. D. and Kirby, L. K. (2000), *Introduction to Type Dynamics and Development: Exploring the Next Level of Type*, Oxford: OPP.

27 Quenk, N. L. (2000), *In The Grip: Understanding Type, Stress, and the Inferior Function*, 2nd edn, Oxford: OPP; Quenk, N. L. (2002), *Was That Really Me? How Everyday Stress Brings out Our Hidden Personality*, Mountain View, CA: Davies-Black.

28 Keating, C. J. (1991), *Who We Are is How We Pray: Matching Personality and Spirituality*, Mystic, CT: Twenty-Third Publications.

29 Duncan, B. (1993), *Pray Your Way: Your Personality and God*, London: Darton, Longman & Todd.

30 Fowke, R. (2008), *Personality and Prayer: Finding the Prayer Style That Suits You*, Farnham: CWR.

31 McGuinness, J. (2009), *Growing Spiritually with the Myers-Briggs® Model*, London: SPCK.

Further reading

Barr, L. and Barr, N. (1993), *The Leadership Equation: Leadership, Management and the Myers-Briggs*, Austin, TX: Eakin Press.

Bayne, R. (2004), *Psychological Types at Work: An MBTI Perspective*, London: Thomson Learning.

Briggs Myers, I. with Myers, P. B. (1995), *Gifts Differing: Understanding Personality Type*, Mountain View, CA: Davies-Black.

Briggs Myers, I., rev. Kirby, L. K. and Myers, K. D. (2000), *Introduction to Type*, Oxford: OPP.

Davies, D., Watkins, C. and Winter, M. (1991), *Church and Religion in Rural England*, Edinburgh: T. & T. Clark.

Duncan, B. (1993), *Pray Your Way: Your Personality and God*, London: Darton, Longman & Todd.

European Province of the Society of Saint Francis (1998), *Celebrating Common Prayer*, London: Mowbray.

Fowke, R. (2008), *Personality and Prayer: Finding the Prayer Style that Suits You*, Farnham: CWR.

Francis, L. J. (2005), *Faith and Psychology: Personality, Religion and the Individual*, London: Darton, Longman & Todd.

Francis, L. J. and Village, A. (2008), *Preaching With All Our Souls: A Study in Hermeneutics and Psychological Type*, London: Continuum.

Goldsmith, M. and Wharton, M. (1993), *Knowing Me, Knowing You: Exploring Personality Type and Temperament*, London: SPCK.

Jung, C. G. (1992), *Psychological Types*, Oxford: Routledge.

Keating, C. J. (1991), *Who We Are is How We Pray: Matching Personality and Spirituality*, Mystic, CT: Twenty-Third Publications.

Keirsey, D. (1998), *Please Understand Me II: Temperament, Character, Intelligence*, Del Mar, CA: Prometheus Nemesis.

Kroeger, O. and Thuesen, J. M. (1988), *TypeTalk: The 16 Personality Types That Determine How We Live, Love, and Work*, New York: Dell.

251

Kummerow, J. M., Barger, N. J. and Kirby, L. K. (1997), *Work Types: Understand Your Work Personality*, New York: Hachette.

Lawrence, G. D. (2009), *People Types and Tiger Stripes: Using Psychological Type to Help Students Discover their Unique Potential*, 4th edn, Gainesville, FL: Center for Applications of Psychological Type.

Lee, C. and Horsman, S. (2002), *Affirmation and Accountability: The Society of Mary and Martha's Manual of Practical Suggestions for Preventing Clergy Stress, Sickness and Ill-Health Retirement*, Exeter: The Society of Mary and Martha.

Leech, K. (ed.) (1996), *Myers-Briggs: Some Critical Reflections*, Manchester: Blackfriars Publications.

McGuinness, J. (2009), *Growing Spiritually with the Myers-Briggs® Model*, London: SPCK.

Northumbria Community Trust (2000), *Celtic Daily Prayer: Prayers and Readings From the Northumbria Community*, London: HarperCollins.

Oswald, R. M. and Kroeger, O. (1988), *Personality Type and Religious Leadership*, Washington, DC: Alban Institute.

Pearman, R. R. and Albritton, S. C. (1997), *I'm Not Crazy, I'm Just Not You: The Real Meaning of the 16 Personality Types*, Mountain View, CA: Davies-Black.

Quenk, N. L. (2002), *Was That Really Me? How Everyday Stress Brings out Our Hidden Personality*, Mountain View, CA: Davies-Black.

Rogers, J. (2007a), *Sixteen Personality Types: At Work in Organisations*, London: Management Futures.

Rogers, J. (2007b), *Influencing Others Using the Sixteen Personality Types*, London: Management Futures.

Did you know that SPCK
is a registered charity?

As well as publishing great books by leading Christian authors, we also . . .

. . . make assemblies meaningful and fun for over a million children by running www.assemblies.org.uk, a popular website that provides free assembly scripts for teachers. For many children, school assembly is the only contact they have with Christian faith and culture, and the only time in their week for spiritual reflection.

. . . help prisoners to become confident readers with our easy-to-read stories. Poor literacy is a huge barrier to rehabilitation. Prisoners identify with the believable heroes of our gritty fiction. At the same time, questions at the end of each chapter help them to examine their choices from a moral perspective and to build their reading confidence.

. . . support student ministers overseas in their training through partnerships in the Global South.

Please support these great schemes: visit www.spck.org.uk/support-us to find out more.